"I'm obsessed with Jessica Merchant's cookbook *Easy Everyday*. It's full of delicious and easy-to-follow recipes that are perfect for any night of the week. The Pistachio Pie Chia Pudding and Hummus Crunch Bowls are just a couple of the dishes I'm dying to try!"

—GINA HOMOLKA, CREATOR OF SKINNYTASTE AND AUTHOR OF THE SKINNYTASTE COOKBOOKS

"Jessica Merchant's new cookbook *Easy Everyday* is all about making delish, memorable meals without breaking a sweat. This book has become my new BFF in the kitchen because I love her approach to whipping up dishes that can be prepped in just ten minutes and ready in thirty. With creative ingredients and fun twists like her zesty Cilantro Lime Grilled Chicken Bowl or her savory French Onion Dutch Baby, you'll never hear the family moan 'this again?' Instead your fam will be begging for seconds because it's all so dang on good."

— JOCELYN DELK ADAMS, BESTSELLING AUTHOR OF *EVERYDAY GRAND: SOULFUL RECIPES FOR CELEBRATING LIFE'S BIG AND SMALL MOMENTS*

"Th   nner dilemma has been solved! *Easy Everyday* is packed with endless mouthwatering recipes and meal prep strategies to create easy-to-prepare dishes (and, hallelujah, leftovers too). Page after page will remind you why it's fun to be in the kitchen so you can have a bounty of food that you can't wait to eat!"

—CATHERINE McCORD, FOUNDER OF WEELICIOUS AND AUTHOR OF *MEAL PREP MAGIC*

"As someone who has been cooking Jessica's recipes for well over a decade now, I consider myself an expert on her recipes and I can say this: they all *deliver*. They're super flavorful, so dang fun, and approachable in the best possible way. I am extra excited about *Easy Everyday* because the thought of being able to obtain Jessica-level flavor on crazy busy weekdays is a dream come true. Smashburger salads?! Get at me!!"

—MOLLY YEH, FOOD NETWORK HOST AND *NEW YORK TIMES* BESTSELLING AUTHOR

easy
everyday

easy everyday

100 recipes and meal prep ideas for effortless eats

jessica merchant

RODALE
NEW YORK

By Jessica Merchant
Easy Everyday
Everyday Dinners
The Pretty Dish
Seriously Delish

Published in the United States by Rodale Books, an imprint
of Random House, a division of Penguin Random House LLC,
New York.

RODALE & Plant colophon is a registered trademark of
Penguin Random House LLC.

LIBRARY OF CONGRESS CATALOGING-IN-PUBLICATION DATA
Names: Merchant, Jessica, author.
Title: Easy everyday / Jessica Merchant.
Description: First edition. | New York, NY: Rodale, [2025] |
Includes index.
Identifiers: LCCN 2024016314 (print) | LCCN 2024016315 (ebook) |
ISBN 9780593796351 (hardcover) | ISBN 9780593796368 (ebook)
Subjects: LCSH: Quick and easy cooking.
Classification: LCC TX833.5 .M489 2025 (print) | LCC TX833.5
(ebook) | DDC 641.5/12—dc23/eng/20240517
LC record available at https://lccn.loc.gov/2024016314
LC ebook record available at https://lccn.loc.gov/2024016315

Printed in China

RodaleBooks.com | RandomHouseBooks.com

9 8 7 6 5 4 3 2 1

First Edition

Book design by Amy Sly, The Sly Studio

Photography by Jessica Merchant

This book is dedicated to all my fellow food lovers: the ones with little time who love to spend it in the kitchen, the ones who love to dance to Whitney and Mariah while they roast a chicken, the ones who eat chocolate chips off of peanut butter spoons, the ones who add crushed chips to their sandwiches, and especially the ones who can't imagine their broccoli without a heavy-handed shower of Parmesan.

contents

chapter 3
lunch loves 81

chapter 4
dinner & sides 107

chapter 5
easy entertaining & snacks 173

chapter 6
treats, treats, treats
199

chapter 7
cocktails & mocktails
227

introduction

Close your eyes. Now imagine this: You've spent your whole day on the beach, and now you're freshly showered, sun-kissed, and no longer salty. The dinner that awaits you starts with stone crabs and melted butter. Warm, garlicky lobster rolls, crisp asparagus, lemony arugula, and truffle fries. Chilled prosecco and raspberry sorbet complete the meal, with just one square of dark chocolate.

Or maybe you're on the bleachers, cheering on your favorite sports team, sitting next to a thermos filled with spiked peppermint hot chocolate, eating melty cheese nachos and snacking on homemade trail mix.

Or you've just stepped outside onto a deck overlooking trees and sparkling water, with streams of sunlight shining down through the branches before the sun dips for the evening. Peppers and halloumi are on the grill; a giant bowl of hot pasta tossed with pesto and Parmesan cheese is waiting for you. An icy, chilled glass of sauvignon blanc is calling your name.

My choice? I'd be transported in time to a cozy kitchen with glittering lights, the smell of warm garlic butter and fresh bread, braised short ribs, and roasted carrots wafting through the air. The table is set, Michael Bublé croons through the speakers, and a wooden bowl piled high with salad greens is just waiting for the drizzle of dressing. Salted maple old-fashioneds are on the menu, complete with gooey caramel cookies.

Food is my favorite form of nourishing, cozy comfort. But it's always who I'm with—who shares the meal with me—that stands out most in my mind.

Food has meant so many different things to me over the years. But there is one constant that reigns supreme: tradition. Tradition and family heritage, leaving a legacy to those I love through recipes. Feeding their bodies but also their souls, making memories with each bite. All with easy, uncomplicated, favorite recipes.

When I think back to my childhood, one of the strongest memories I have is being around the table. I see flashes of our weeknight dinners, where my mom made tacos every Monday night and chicken marsala every Wednesday. The times I'd snort water through my nose because my brothers made me laugh so hard, and even my parents couldn't contain the giggles.

I see my grandmother's table, complete with her frozen cranberry salad on tiny plates to the left and demitasse cups to the right, along with a stack of peppermint swizzle sticks for after-dinner coffee.

Or my mom's fancy dining room that she'd set up for her card club—the club that still meets to this day, fifty years later. I can still see the wax from taper candles dripping on the tablecloth and empty glasses with the remains of Baileys Irish Cream, plates scraped clean from her Oreo ice cream dessert.

Nothing is quite as strong as the memories of the dinners we had together daily, the dishes my mom made embedded in my brain. How she appeared to serve us with ease and comfort, even on the rare occasion that it was scrambled eggs or cereal for dinner. It still felt like family dinner.

The memories of these meals that my family enjoyed together—the classic, traditional dishes that have been the base inspiration for so many of my own creations—evoke emotions in my heart that scream love, joy, togetherness, and family heritage. It's those moments, memories, and recipes that inspired me to put together a book for you filled with easy everyday recipes. Recipes that can make your life easier while at the same time provide togetherness and shared love around the table each day and night.

That's exactly what I aim for today. I want my whole family and especially my kids, to remember our moments together around the table with intense joy. Delicious food is my gateway to the heart and soul of those I love. Especially when it's easy.

I can not only hear and feel the memories, I can *taste* them.

Over the years, my family managed to create these memories with uncomplicated, unfussy, fabulous recipes that have stood the test of time. It has always inspired me to create recipes that are simple but memorable, easy but unique, classic with a modern twist.

Alas, all dreaminess aside, today the world is bonkers. Every day is fast-paced and busy, and it feels like we are always racing to the next thing. I'm a product of the internet generation, where I have been able to access everything almost instantly. But I'm lucky enough to also remember those days (and meals!) where things were enjoyed, consumed, and cooked slowly and deliberately.

So, it means something to me to take the time to prepare a meal. The thing is, I just don't always *have* that time. Who does?

Sure, I love taking my time in the kitchen every now and then. I pop on a killer playlist, grab a glass of wine, and take my good old time to impart flavor into a meal that will take more than an hour to come together. But it's not feasible for everyday life. So, every single meal—and I'm talking breakfast, lunch, and dinner—must check a few boxes for me.

The first box? The meals must be approachable. I don't want to think *too* much when I glance at a recipe. The last thing I want is to be stressed out.

Next, I also only want dinners to take me about 30 to 45 minutes to make, preferably even less. Sure there is the occasional meal that takes around an hour, and you'll find just a handful of those here. Breakfasts and lunches have to come together almost instantly, unless it's a special occasion or I find myself with a luxurious chunk of time. Weekend specials aside.

Of course, I want everything to taste delicious! Sounds ridiculous, but it's a must.

Finally, I especially want to serve easy, balanced meals and dishes that nourish my family's bodies and souls, with an occasional indulgence here and there.

I don't think this is too much to ask for, but it isn't always accessible. So, I'm here for you! I've got you.

So, I've put together this cookbook of favorite recipes, from the things we eat at breakfast to the drinks we consume after dinner. Recipes that taste wonderful and special enough that your family remembers them and requests them. But recipes that are also easy enough that you don't want to pull your hair out.

I'll tell you how I make these meals with a few minutes of meal prep here and there, and the secrets I have for getting meals on the table, whether it's morning, noon, or night.

how i approach menu planning with the big three

When it comes to menu planning for a week ahead, nothing sounds worse to me than having five containers filled with the exact same protein, grain, and vegetable for the week. That is a recipe for boredom, and boredom is what drives my recipe brain. It's the reason I like to create recipes—to stave off that boredom.

But I don't want to loathe preplanned meals either.

I want everything to taste great. Fresh! Inspiring!

Because of that, I look at menu planning with what I call **the big three**.

I choose three ingredients that can work three different ways. And there are three things I look for in these ingredients.

1. versatility
2. ease of preparation
3. leftover quality

I want these ingredients to be able to fit a variety of different meals, in different ways. I want each meal to taste different, which is where **versatility** comes in for me.

However, I don't want to spend all day in the kitchen on a weeknight preparing food ahead of time. The **ease of preparation** is KEY here. I want the ingredients to be something I can prepare quickly, or at least gives me a lot of downtime when I'm preparing it.

I rarely think meals taste better as leftovers (chili, taco meat, and many dips aside), but I certainly want to make sure that the ingredients I prepare for the week will have **high-quality leftovers**. Because, of course, I want things to taste good! I want to be excited about every meal. Life is too short not to be thrilled with everything we eat.

Here's an example of three ingredients that I use often. They all fit the bill for my big three.

Whole roasted chicken: I've often wished that someone would make a "whole roasted chicken" candle for the single reason that it makes your home smell like heaven. It's also super easy to prepare! I throw a whole chicken on a roasting pan, shower it in salt and olive oil (see my easy recipe on page 108), and let it roast for around an hour and a half. While this is the ingredient that takes the longest for me to prepare, the prep time is almost all downtime. And the options are endless! Soups, enchiladas, stuffed peppers—you can't go wrong here.

A big batch of pearl couscous. This goes for any pasta, rice, grain (or anything that acts as a grain!), or similar ingredients. A large batch takes anywhere from 15 to 40 minutes and can be used in endless ways, from a plain side dish to a breakfast base or stuffed in vegetables. And a pro tip: I like to cook my couscous in bone broth. Not only does it up the flavor, but it also adds a good amount of protein and, therefore, satiety.

An adaptable dressing or sauce, like my Green Goddess Ranch (page 26) or Sun-Dried Tomato Pesto (page 34). Sauces and dressings like these are a great way to add variety and flavor to just about any meal. Aside from being used in their traditional way, these can be stirred into grains, used as a drizzle for eggs or a spread for sandwiches, as well as a dip for vegetables or a base for pizza. Again, this allows for countless dinner options. And that makes all of us very happy.

some meal prep secrets that changed my life

Not to sound dramatic, but these really *have* changed my life.

I cover many of these secrets in my book *Everyday Dinners*, but they make such a huge difference that they are worth mentioning again.

10-Minute Meal Prep Is a Real Thing

It sounds kind of crazy. But I can accomplish MULTIPLE things for a meal in 10 minutes. I can make a dressing and chop an onion for later. I can measure out ingredients and set them aside. I can make a simple syrup. I swear this saves me so much time and allows us to eat more balanced, nutritious meals.

I wash and chop/store vegetables ahead of time

This is huge for us, because it makes for easy grab-and-go vegetables for soups and side dishes. And for snacking, too. This only takes a few minutes and has a large impact on our weekly meals.

I mix up whatever I can ahead of time

This means dressings, sauces (including caramel sauce!), chia pudding, and even Bolognese. It also means I marinate meat or vegetables when I can. I'm always trying to think of what I can do **now** instead of later. And my future self always thanks me.

my 10-minute meal prep strategy

I first told you about this concept in my book *Everyday Dinners*. It has been a lifesaver for me, especially since having kids. Using my 10-minute meal prep strategy has allowed me to cook dinners for my family almost every night, mostly stress-free.

I say "mostly" because I am human. You know?

But it's not just dinner. This strategy also allows me to have easy, satisfying, and healthy snacks and lunches on hand for everyone. Including myself! And it also allows me to have breakfasts prepared, too, whether fully made or halfway prepped for something special on the weekend.

While this strategy doesn't sound like it could make a huge difference, the compound effect is significant. By chopping some vegetables ahead of time, or making a vinaigrette for your favorite salad, marinating some chicken, and even cooking a batch of couscous—the time you gain is powerful.

We live in a time where every moment counts, and I find that to be especially true for those dinnertime hours. That chunk of time between four P.M. and eight P.M., when you're starting to feel the exhaustion of the day but trying to manage the schedules of every living thing in your home (human, plant, animal—they all count!). Those are the hours when this tiny bit of prep helps the most.

You can release the anxiety of ingredient prepping because that part of dinner is mostly done. The thought of packing breakfasts and lunches for the next day may also be taken care of.

This small but mighty strategy will save you time, energy, and brainpower in the long run. It's one thing that I never, ever regret doing!

Every recipe in this book contains a note for where you can implement 10 minutes of meal prep. Sometimes the entire recipe can be made ahead of time, in just 10 minutes! But most of the time, there are one or two things that can be prepped in that timeframe. I find that sometimes it works for me to do those few minutes of prep while I'm making tonight's dinner, when the kitchen is already strewn with ingredients and dishes have to be done. Other days, I set aside a few minutes in the morning to throw together a quick marinade or to measure out the ingredients for that evening's dinner.

I can't wait until you try it and notice the difference! ●

what i keep in the pantry & fridge for easy meals

O All-purpose flour

O Beans—garbanzo, black, and cannellini

O Bread crumbs—panko and fine; I like using seasoned varieties when possible

O Canned tomatoes—fire roasted, crushed, and diced

O Condiments—Dijon, yellow, and grainy mustards; mayonnaise

O Dry grains—rice, quinoa, couscous, and farro top my list

O Kosher salt and black pepper

O Nuts—sliced almonds, pine nuts, walnuts, pistachios, and cashews

O Oils—extra-virgin olive, avocado, chili, coconut, canola, and toasted sesame

O Pasta—short-cut and long noodles

O Puff pastry

O Sauces—such as jarred marinara, Worcestershire, and soy

O Spices and dried herbs—garlic powder, smoked paprika, cumin, chili powder, and crushed red pepper flakes

O Stock and broth—chicken, vegetable, and beef

O Sweeteners—brown sugar, granulated sugar, honey, and maple syrup

O Tomato paste and anchovy paste

O Tuna packed in olive oil

O Vinegars—apple cider, red wine, and champagne are my favorite varieties

O Wine—dry white and full-bodied red

meat temperature safety guide

POULTRY	
White Meat	160°F, 71°C
Dark Meat	165°F, 75°C
Ground Poultry	165°F, 75°C
PORK	
White Meat	145°F, 63°C
Dark Meat	160°F, 71°C
Ground Pork	160°F, 71°C
BEEF	
Rare	120°F, 40°C
Medium-Rare	130°F, 55°C
Medium	140°F, 60°C
Medium-Well	150°F, 63°C
Well Done	160°F, 71°C

important cooking things that can't be overlooked

How I use salt

In almost all my recipes, I suggest you add a big pinch of salt (and black pepper) to the dish when cooking. This is something I strongly believe in, because it teaches you how to become a better cook. It encourages you to taste your food and learn to cook based on how it tastes, instead of just blindly following a recipe.

My favorite salt is Diamond Crystal Kosher Salt and I have it out at all times. Adjusting the salt to your taste in a recipe can be tricky because different salts have different "salty" flavors. Some are saltier than others! I created all of the recipes in this book with Diamond Crystal Kosher Salt in mind.

Seasoning to taste can be stressful for some people, so you can always start with ¼ or ½ teaspoon of salt and taste from there, adjusting accordingly. Some things require a bigger pinch of salt (like salad dressings, breads, pasta water, even lettuce greens) while others can manage with ½ teaspoon). The more you cook, the more you learn!

How I use lemon

I really love to use lemon in my cooking. A splash of acid can be a game changer in a dish and bring out so many flavors. There are many recipes that use lemon in this book, but that doesn't mean they all taste like lemon.

The next time you feel like a recipe is missing something, add a squeeze of fresh lemon juice and see how it changes things. It enhances the flavor and brightens the dish.

How I toast nuts

Many of my recipes call for toasted nuts, such as pine nuts, almonds, or walnuts. I love the depth of flavor that toasted nuts bring to a dish, not to mention the wonderful texture and crunch. The buttery flavor is unmatched!

To easily toast nuts on the stovetop, I place them in a skillet over medium-low heat. Do not walk away! They burn so quickly—the key is to shake the pan every few seconds and stir with a wooden spoon until the nuts are toasty. Once they are golden in color, I immediately remove them from the heat and dump them in a bowl or on a plate to stop the cooking.

You can also toast nuts in the oven on a baking sheet. I do this at 350°F for around 10 minutes or so. Watch them closely! Some may take less time.

Parmesan rinds are your friend

I have a container of Parmesan rinds in my freezer at all times. In fact, I usually have two containers and it still doesn't feel like enough. I use Parmesan rinds to flavor just about every single soup I make. There is such a difference in flavor when you add Parmesan to broth. It imparts a nutty, salty essence that you can't find elsewhere. It is key.

Many stores these days have containers of Parmesan rinds at the cheese counter that you can buy. But to start your own stockpile, simply buy a wedge of Parmesan cheese and slice off the rind. Store it in a resealable container or bag in the freezer for up to 6 months.

And you should shave cheese over salads and soups

My favorite way to enjoy cheese in a salad or on top of a hot soup is by shaving shards of it over said bowls.

I love how paper-thin the cheese pieces are. In salads, they get mixed up with the lettuce and you find salty, savory bits in each bite. With soups, they melt like a very thin blanket over parts of the bowl, and you get an accidental-on-purpose cheese pull.

You can buy shaved Parmesan cheese at the grocery store. But you can also easily use a vegetable peeler to shave slices of it yourself. This is what I do for my Shaved Asiago House Salad (page 125) and it's wonderful.

puff pastry is a staple ingredient

And that's no exaggeration. We love puff pastry in this house SO much, and I use it for many different recipes: pizzas, appetizers, pot pie crust, desserts, and more. It's incredibly easy to work with and it cooks rather quickly, so I have it on hand at all times.

I prefer to buy the pastry that comes in one long sheet—it does not have perforations in it—and it's actually refrigerated with the pie dough instead of in the freezer section. It's the best kind to work with and very easy to use!

six tools i can't live without

Nutribullet

Or really any small, personal blender that can hold about 16 ounces. This is probably my most used kitchen appliance, and it gets a workout multiple times a week. I do not use this for smoothies, but I do use it for dressings and sauces. It emulsifies dressings so incredibly well and blends things like ranch and Caesar dressings easily and quickly. It's not as cumbersome as dragging out a large blender or food processor. And it's very easy to clean, too.

Microplane

Many of my recipes call for fresh lime zest, and some call for lemon and orange zest, too. I love how much zip and flavor citrus zest can add to a recipe, so I always have a Microplane or two on hand for this reason. Additionally, I sometimes use it to grate ginger and garlic.

Citrus juicer

On that same note, I love a large citrus juicer or press that can make multiple ounces of juice at a time. My favorite one is made by Smeg and it is used in my kitchen frequently. It's also wonderful to bring out on holidays or for cocktails that require fresh citrus juice.

Mezzaluna

This curved knife with handles is my go-to piece of equipment for slicing pizzas, chopping herbs, and making chopped salads. I use it multiple days a week, and it makes things so much easier in the kitchen.

Serrated grapefruit spoons

I use these for citrus, of course. But what I use these for most often is to scrape the seeds out of fall and winter squash. Think butternut, acorn, spaghetti squash, and pumpkins. Serrated spoons make it so easy to remove the seeds.

Meat thermometer

I use mine nearly every single day, to ensure that my chicken is cooked thoroughly enough and to make sure that I don't overdo the steak. This is a must-have in everyone's kitchen! ●

Caprese Cottage Cheese Toast (page 92)

CHAPTER 1

sauces &
dressings

aka my fridge essentials

These little recipes right here, the ones in this chapter that kick off the book, are the ones that save my meal-prepping life.

Okay, that may be a bit dramatic, but it's partially true. My favorite way to elevate a meal, make it feel special, fancy, or most important, *different*, is by adding a dressing or a sauce. Sometimes this can be in the form of a marinade, whether it's for meat, seafood, or even vegetables. In other instances, this may be a simple salad dressing or dipping sauce. My vinaigrettes and dressings can be made ahead of time and stored in the fridge, making them the perfect candidate for your 10-minute meal prep.

It's up to you how many of these recipes you may prep in a week, but I'll spill my secrets: I like to prepare two or three, and usually make sure that they have some versatility within the meals I am planning to make.

This means that I might prepare my Cilantro Lime Dressing (page 29) for marinating chicken. But I will also make a batch of Green Goddess Ranch (page 26) because it's perfect for dipping and drizzling. It will extend the life of the meal and make the leftovers taste slightly different, but still delicious!

My Chili Pepita Crunch (page 47) is fabulous on tacos, but also wonderful on a breakfast bowl of crispy rice and fried eggs (see page 73). My Go-To Zesty Italian Dressing (page 44) makes a fabulous marinade but also works on any salad. Making the Sun-Dried Tomato Pesto (page 34)? Use it as pizza sauce or drizzle it over roasted sweet potatoes. The options are endless.

Because I'm all about the variety over here. It's the spice of (meal-prepping) life! ●

caramelized shallot dressing

caramelized shallots

1 tablespoon extra-virgin olive oil

6 medium shallots, peeled and thinly sliced horizontally

Kosher salt

½ teaspoon baking soda

vinaigrette

3 tablespoons apple cider vinegar

1 teaspoon honey

2 garlic cloves, finely minced or pressed

Kosher salt and black pepper

Pinch of crushed red pepper flakes

½ cup extra-virgin olive oil

If you're a lover of caramelized onions, this dressing is for you. It's incredible on my Smashburger Salad (page 134) and fabulous on roasted vegetables or grilled meats. It's even wonderful drizzled on garlic bread. It does take a little extra prep work because the shallots need time to caramelize, so keep that in mind.

make the caramelized shallots   Heat the olive oil in a skillet over medium heat. Add the sliced shallots and a big pinch of salt. Add the baking soda. Cook for about 5 minutes, until the shallots start to soften and brown. Reduce the heat to medium-low. Cook for another 15 minutes or so, stirring often, reducing the heat if needed, until deeply golden in color and caramelized. Don't let them burn!

make the vinaigrette   Whisk together the vinegar, honey, garlic, salt, pepper, and red pepper flakes. Continue to whisk while streaming in the olive oil. Stir in the caramelized shallots. This dressing stays great in the fridge for up to 5 days. It's best when brought back to room temperature for serving, so remove it from the fridge 1 hour before using.

green goddess ranch

1 cup plain Greek yogurt or sour cream

1 cup packed spinach leaves

½ cup mayonnaise

½ cup whole milk

3 tablespoons fresh chives or 1 tablespoon dried chives

2 tablespoons fresh dill or 2 teaspoons dried dill

1 tablespoon fresh parsley or 1 teaspoon dried parsley

2 teaspoons fresh lemon juice

1 teaspoon garlic powder

½ teaspoon onion powder

¼ teaspoon smoked paprika

Kosher salt and black pepper

The ranch dressing to end all ranch dressings! This is my absolute favorite ranch recipe, and the extra pop of green from the spinach and herbs make it beautiful. It's herbaceous, delicious, and ideal for dipping, drizzling, or spreading.

Combine the yogurt, spinach, mayo, milk, chives, dill, parsley, lemon juice, garlic powder, onion powder, paprika, and a big pinch of salt and pepper in a blender. Blend until the dressing is smooth and creamy. Taste and add more salt and pepper as you feel necessary. This is a great dressing to make ahead of time. It will stay fresh in a sealed container in the fridge for up to 5 days.

hot ginger dressing

1 tablespoon toasted sesame oil

1 small shallot, diced

Kosher salt

2 tablespoons chopped fresh ginger

1 garlic clove, minced

1½ tablespoons red wine or apple cider vinegar

1 tablespoon honey

1 teaspoon soy sauce

⅓ cup extra-virgin olive oil

My hot ginger dressing was inspired by my grandma's love for hot bacon dressing. I took the same idea but instead used sizzled ginger, and the end result is incredible. I love this on salads and even drizzled on potatoes.

Heat the sesame oil in a saucepan over medium-low heat. Stir in the shallot with a pinch of salt and cook until soft, about 2 minutes. Stir in the ginger and garlic and cook for 1 to 2 minutes more. Reduce the heat to low. Whisk in the vinegar, honey, and soy sauce. Whisk in the olive oil until emulsified.

Serve the dressing warm over your favorite salad. This can be stored in the fridge for up to 3 days. When ready to use, transfer it to a saucepan and reheat.

piccata vinaigrette

3 tablespoons red wine vinegar

3 tablespoons diced shallots

3 tablespoons capers

1 teaspoon lemon zest

1 tablespoon lemon juice

3 garlic cloves, minced

Kosher salt and black pepper

½ cup extra-virgin olive oil

If you need a way to fancy up your vegetables or meat, give this piccata vinaigrette a try! Tangy lemon, salty capers, and umami garlic bring a ridiculous amount of flavor to any meal. My favorite way to use this is on my roasted chicken and potatoes (page 131).

Whisk together the vinegar, shallots, capers, lemon zest and juice, garlic, and a big pinch of salt and pepper. Whisk in the olive oil until emulsified. Taste and season more, if desired. This can be stored in a sealed container in the fridge for 3 or 4 days.

brown butter vinaigrette

4 tablespoons unsalted butter

1 garlic clove, minced

1 tablespoon champagne vinegar

2 teaspoons freshly squeezed lemon juice

½ teaspoon Dijon mustard

½ teaspoon kosher salt

Freshly cracked black pepper to taste

2 tablespoons grapeseed or avocado oil

This vinaigrette is extra savory and rich with a hint of caramel flavor thanks to the brown butter. This is such a versatile staple. It's best served warm and is excellent on grilled chicken, rice or grains, roasted vegetables, and of course, salad.

Place the butter in a small saucepan over medium heat and immediately begin whisking as it melts. Stir as it bubbles, and after 2 to 3 minutes you should see brown bits appear on the bottom of the pan. Remove from the heat immediately, add the garlic, and continue to whisk for another 30 seconds.

Whisk in the champagne vinegar, lemon juice, mustard, salt, pepper, and oil. You can let the dressing cool slightly, but it's most delicious when served warm! Whisk it occasionally when serving because a bit of separation is normal. This stays good in the fridge for up to 3 days. Transfer it to a saucepan to reheat it before serving.

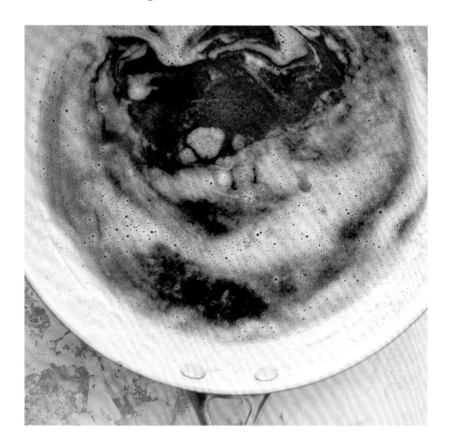

cilantro lime dressing

3 tablespoons freshly squeezed lime juice

1½ tablespoons honey

¼ cup fresh cilantro

2 garlic cloves, minced or pressed

¼ teaspoon kosher salt

¼ teaspoon black pepper

Pinch of crushed red pepper flakes

⅓ cup extra-virgin olive oil

I can barely go a week without making this vibrant green dressing. It's a fabulous marinade and dressing, and I also love to stir a few spoonfuls into cooked quinoa or couscous.

In a blender or food processor, combine the lime juice, honey, cilantro, garlic, salt, pepper, red pepper flakes, and olive oil. Blend until combined and smooth (some pieces of cilantro may remain). Leftovers stay great in the fridge for a few days! Store it in a sealed container.

smashed feta vinaigrette

3 tablespoons red wine vinegar

2 tablespoons freshly squeezed lemon juice

2 teaspoons honey

Kosher salt and black pepper

2 tablespoons chopped fresh dill

2 tablespoons chopped fresh chives

⅓ cup crumbled feta cheese

½ cup extra-virgin olive oil

If you're looking for a dressing that will make a dish pop, this is it. My smashed feta vinaigrette has hints of lemon and dill, lots of crumbled feta, and red wine vinegar. It tastes classic but unique; familiar but new. I love it on traditional greens salads but enjoy it the most on pasta salad.

In a bowl, whisk together the vinegar, lemon juice, honey, salt, pepper, herbs, and feta. Use a spoon or whisk to smash some of the feta into the mixture. Whisk the olive oil into the dressing until combined. You can make this ahead of time and store it in the fridge for up to 5 days. It will separate over time, but whisking or shaking will bring it back together.

i adore this balsamic dressing

4 garlic cloves, minced

2 tablespoons balsamic vinegar

1½ tablespoons Dijon mustard

1 tablespoon granulated sugar

1 teaspoon dried oregano

Kosher salt and black pepper

½ cup extra-virgin olive oil

This balsamic dressing is life-changing. It's thick and syrupy without being overly sweet, and it clings to salad greens and pasta noodles alike. It has fabulous flavor and is also a great dressing for anything that comes off the grill: vegetables, breads, meats, and seafood.

Whisk together the garlic, vinegar, mustard, sugar, oregano, and a big pinch of salt and pepper. Whisk in the olive oil until the mixture is thickened and emulsified. This can be made ahead of time and stored in the fridge in a sealed container until ready to use! It will stay good for up to 1 week. Just whisk or shake before using.

honey mustard vinaigrette

3 tablespoons apple cider vinegar

2 tablespoons honey

1 tablespoon Dijon mustard

2 garlic cloves, finely minced or pressed

¼ teaspoon kosher salt

¼ teaspoon black pepper

½ cup extra-virgin olive oil

Honey mustard will always hold a special place in my heart. I'm sure it stems from my love of chicken nuggets dipped in honey mustard as a child. Well, I'm glad to tell you that this is how we elevate it. A honey mustard vinaigrette—not a super thick and creamy sauce—gives honey mustard a glow up. It's a win for everyone.

In a bowl, whisk together the vinegar, honey, mustard, garlic, salt, and pepper. Continue to whisk while streaming in the olive oil. This dressing stays great in the fridge in a sealed container for about 1 week.

citrus vinaigrette

1 teaspoon freshly grated
orange zest

2 tablespoons freshly squeezed
orange juice

1 tablespoon red wine vinegar

1 teaspoon honey

1 teaspoon Dijon mustard

1 garlic clove, finely minced
or pressed

¼ teaspoon kosher salt

¼ teaspoon black pepper

½ cup extra-virgin olive oil

This citrus vinaigrette is one of my classics. I love it in winter, when it's peak citrus season, but it's also fantastic any time of year when you just need a "really good dressing."

Whisk together the orange zest and juice, vinegar, honey, mustard, garlic, salt, pepper, and olive oil until combined and emulsified. This dressing lasts in the fridge for 3 to 4 days in a sealed container.

champagne vinaigrette

3 tablespoons champagne vinegar

½ lemon, juiced

2 tablespoons honey

1 teaspoon Dijon mustard

1 garlic clove, grated

Kosher salt and black pepper

½ cup extra-virgin olive oil

Another one of my staples, champagne vinaigrette is what I turn to when I find apple cider to be too tangy and red wine to taste too familiar. Champagne vinegar has a bit of a lighter flavor, and it's a wonderful neutral dressing to use on just about anything. It's the dressing to make when you don't know what dressing to make.

Combine the vinegar, lemon juice, honey, mustard, garlic, and a pinch of salt and pepper in a large bowl and whisk together. Stream in the olive oil while constantly whisking until the dressing comes together. Store in the fridge for up to 1 week in a sealed container.

lemon caesar dressing

4 garlic cloves, minced

3 tablespoons plain Greek yogurt

2 tablespoons finely grated Parmesan cheese

1 tablespoon Dijon mustard

2 teaspoons red wine vinegar

1 teaspoon anchovy paste

2 teaspoons freshly grated lemon zest

½ lemon, juiced

Kosher salt and black pepper

⅓ cup extra-virgin olive oil

Caesar dressing is my love language. Add some extra lemon and it climbs higher on the list. This is fabulous on salads, wraps, pizza, and more.

Add the garlic, yogurt, Parmesan, mustard, vinegar, anchovy paste, lemon zest and juice, and a big pinch of salt and pepper to a food processor or blender and blend until pureed. With the processor still on, stream in the olive oil until a creamy dressing forms. This stays great in the fridge in a sealed container for 3 to 4 days. Stir well before using.

sun-dried tomato pesto

2 (5-ounce) jars sun-dried tomatoes in oil

½ cup fresh basil leaves

⅓ cup freshly grated Parmesan cheese

⅓ cup toasted pine nuts

½ lemon, juiced

1 teaspoon honey

4 garlic cloves

Kosher salt and black pepper

4 to 6 tablespoons extra-virgin olive oil

I love having a red pesto recipe in my life. This is great as a dip or on pasta, pizza, vegetables, or meats. I always have some stored in my freezer!

Place the sun-dried tomatoes and the oil from the jar in the bowl of a food processor. Add the basil, cheese, pine nuts, lemon juice, honey, garlic, and a big pinch of salt and pepper. Pulse and blend until the mixture comes together. Add more olive oil as needed, 1 tablespoon at a time. Taste and season with additional salt and pepper, if desired.

This freezes great in a sealed container for up to 3 months and also stays good in the fridge for up to 1 week.

our all-time favorite basil pesto

4 cups fresh basil leaves

4 garlic cloves

1 cup finely grated Parmesan cheese

½ cup toasted pine nuts

1 teaspoon freshly squeezed lemon juice

Kosher salt and black pepper

½ to ¾ cup extra-virgin olive oil

Basil pesto is something we can't live without. I stockpile it in my freezer at the end of the summer. The uses for it are endless (marinades, stirred into grains, spread on sandwiches, and so on) and it's so easy to make!

Combine the basil, garlic, Parmesan, pine nuts, lemon juice, and a big pinch of salt and pepper in a food processor. Pulse until small crumbs remain and everything is combined. With the processor on, stream in the olive oil until the mixture comes together.

Taste and season with more salt and pepper if needed. Use as desired! This stays good in the fridge for up to 3 days and freezes well, too. Store it in a sealed container in the freezer for up to 3 months. Defrost in the fridge when ready to use. Frozen, individually wrapped cubes defrost super fast in the event of an unplanned visit.

fancy dipping oil that no one can resist

1 tablespoon dried oregano

1 tablespoon dried basil

2 teaspoons minced onions

1 teaspoon dried thyme

1 teaspoon kosher salt

1 teaspoon freshly cracked black pepper

½ teaspoon crushed red pepper flakes

⅓ cup extra-virgin olive oil

4 garlic cloves, minced

1 tablespoon finely grated Parmesan cheese

1 tablespoon balsamic vinegar

2 tablespoons diced green olives

2 tablespoons chopped fresh basil

This dipping oil is outrageous, in the best way possible. Grab your favorite bread and serve this to your friends and family. They may never leave!

Combine the oregano, dried basil, onion, thyme, salt, pepper, and red pepper flakes in a bowl and stir. Add the olive oil, garlic, and Parmesan and stir again. Drizzle in the balsamic vinegar and stir in the diced olives and fresh basil.

Serve with fresh bread for dipping! This keeps great in the fridge for 2 to 3 days.

hummus dressing

½ cup plain hummus, or your favorite variety, such as roasted red pepper, garlic, or even black bean

1 lemon, juiced

2 teaspoons honey

2 teaspoons fresh ginger, grated

Kosher salt and black pepper

5 to 6 tablespoons cold water, around 40°F

We adore hummus in our house and go through it at an alarming rate. One of my favorite uses for it is salad dressing! The flavor that it brings to the dressing, as well as the satiety, is something I really love when it comes to salads. You can easily use your favorite hummus in this recipe, allowing for more variety and fun flavors.

Whisk together the hummus, lemon juice, honey, ginger, and a big pinch of salt and pepper until smooth. Whisk in the water until the mixture smooths and thins out. Taste and adjust seasoning before serving. This can be stored in a sealed container in the fridge for up to 1 week.

quick pickled sweet peppers

1 pound mini sweet peppers, thinly sliced

½ cup warm water, around 115°F

1½ tablespoons sugar

1 teaspoon coarse salt

¾ cup apple cider vinegar

I love sweet pickled peppers on all the things: salads, wraps, or even straight from the jar. These add a pop to any dish (think in tacos, on top of pizza) and you'll never regret having them in your fridge.

Place the sliced peppers in a large mason jar or cup. Set aside.

In a bowl, whisk together the water, sugar, and salt until the sugar and salt dissolve. Whisk in the vinegar. Pour the liquid over the sliced peppers. Let sit uncovered at room temperature for 30 minutes to 1 hour. You can make this ahead of time; once made, store in a sealed container in the fridge. These pickled peppers last for about 1 week.

quick pickled onions

1 medium red onion, thinly sliced

¾ cup apple cider vinegar

1½ tablespoons sugar

1 teaspoon kosher salt

1 cup water

When in doubt, add pickled onions! These quick onions are easy to make and work well in tacos, salads, and grain bowls. They are tangy and flavorful and instantly elevate any dish.

Place the onions in a heatproof jar. Set aside.

Combine the vinegar, sugar, and salt with the water in a saucepan over medium heat. Bring the mixture to a boil, whisking to dissolve the sugar and salt, about 3 minutes. Turn off the heat and pour the mixture over the onions. Let them sit at room temperature to cool.

Once cool, seal the jar and keep in the fridge. These are good for up to 1 week!

seasoned sourdough croutons

12-ounce loaf of sourdough bread, cut into cubes

3 to 4 tablespoons extra-virgin olive oil

1 teaspoon garlic powder

½ teaspoon dried oregano

½ teaspoon dried basil

Kosher salt and black pepper

2 tablespoons finely grated Parmesan cheese

I make these croutons every single week and promptly eat about ten of them right off the pan. They go incredibly well on my asiago salad (page 123) and taste so much better than store-bought croutons.

Preheat the oven to 400°F. Line a baking sheet with parchment paper.

Spread the bread cubes out on the sheet. Drizzle with the olive oil and toss well, until every piece of bread is coated with the oil. Sprinkle the garlic powder, oregano, basil, and a big pinch of salt and pepper all over the bread. Toss many times until evenly coated. Sprinkle with the Parmesan and toss again.

Bake for 8 to 10 minutes, then toss and bake for about 5 minutes more, until golden and crunchy. Remove from the oven and let cool completely. Store in a resealable container or bag for about 1 week.

roasted garlic

2 heads of garlic

2 teaspoons extra-virgin olive oil

Kosher salt

Roasted garlic is as simple as can be. It takes an hour, but it's hands-off time and the end result always leaves you happier than you were before. It tastes like golden, caramelly, garlicky butter.

Preheat the oven to 375°F.

Slice off the top portion of each garlic head to reveal the cloves. Lightly rub back and forth to remove the paper on the sides and peel off any excess paper, keeping the whole garlic head intact. Drizzle about 1 teaspoon of the olive oil on top of each head of garlic. Sprinkle with salt. Wrap the garlic heads in foil together and place the foil pouch on a baking sheet. Roast for 45 minutes. The garlic should be fragrant; and when you unwrap the foil, the cloves should look golden in color.

Let cool until you can touch it. Remove the garlic from the foil. When ready to use, squeeze the garlic cloves out of the head. If you want to make this ahead of time, you can store the whole roasted garlic head in the fridge in a sealed container for up to 3 days.

quick tomato jam

1½ cups whole cherry tomatoes

2 garlic cloves, minced

2 tablespoons sugar

2 tablespoons fresh lime juice

1 teaspoon apple cider vinegar

Kosher salt and black pepper

Quick tomato jam is a must-have for one of my most-made snacks, the Ricotta Jam Jar (page 177). It can also be used on pizza (see page 171) and even as a spread for breakfast sandwiches. It's unique and special, but super easy to make!

In a saucepan over medium heat, combine the tomatoes, garlic, sugar, lime juice, vinegar, and a pinch of salt and pepper. Stir often, cooking until the tomatoes begin to burst, about 8 minutes. Continue to cook as the mixture bubbles and the tomatoes break down, using a wooden spoon to break them apart if needed, 10 to 15 minutes.

If you want the mixture to stay chunky, keep it as it is. If you want it smooth, carefully transfer it to a food processor or blender. A small smoothie blender is perfect for this. Blend until pureed. Pour into a jar and let sit at room temperature until the mixture cools completely. It will thicken more as it cools. Once cool, store in a sealed container in the fridge for up to 3 days.

my go-to zesty italian dressing

¼ cup red wine vinegar

4 garlic cloves, minced

1 tablespoon Dijon mustard

1 tablespoon honey

1 tablespoon dried oregano

1 teaspoon kosher salt

1 teaspoon freshly cracked black pepper

½ cup extra-virgin olive oil

This is the best Italian dressing I've ever had, and, yes, I may be biased. It's a wonderfully classic, super garlicky dressing that transforms any salad with just a small drizzle.

Whisk together the vinegar, garlic, mustard, honey, oregano, salt, and pepper until combined. Stream in the olive oil while whisking until emulsified. This dressing stays great in the fridge for 1 week! Just whisk or shake before serving.

yogurt blue cheese sauce

1 cup plain Greek yogurt

½ lemon, juiced

Kosher salt and black pepper

¾ cup crumbled blue cheese

2 scallions, thinly sliced

1 teaspoon chives

½ teaspoon dried dill

Enter my favorite dipping sauce for any sort of chicken, steak, or grilled vegetable. This sauce is packed with protein and loaded with flavor. It's good enough to eat with a spoon.

Mix together the yogurt, lemon juice, salt, pepper, blue cheese, scallions, chives, and dill in a bowl, mashing in the blue cheese as you stir. Serve immediately! You can make this ahead of time and store it in the fridge for 3 to 4 days.

chili pepita crunch

3 tablespoons roasted pepitas

3 tablespoons dried minced onion

2 tablespoons dried minced garlic

½ cup extra-virgin olive oil

½ to 1 teaspoon kosher salt

2 teaspoons smoked paprika

1 teaspoon crushed red pepper flakes

½ teaspoon chili powder

This spicy, crunchy topping finds its way into many of my meals. Whether I'm dressing up fried eggs or spooning it over Crispy Potato Tacos (page 117), it makes everything it touches taste incredible.

Place the pepitas, onion, and garlic in a bowl. Top with the olive oil. Stir in the salt (I start with ½ teaspoon and adjust as needed), smoked paprika, and red pepper flakes. Taste and add more salt, if desired. Transfer to a 6- or 8-ounce jar.

This is delicious served on top of just about anything! Store it in the fridge for up to 2 weeks.

breakfast bites

Since having children, my breakfast priorities have changed.

First, it needs to be said that I LOVE breakfast. I was never one to skip breakfast, ever. Growing up, when my brothers complained that they weren't hungry before school, I was happily chowing down on bowls of strawberries-and-cream oatmeal, toasted bagels with peanut butter and honey, or even English muffins with scrambled eggs and cheese.

I've always loved breakfast, and it goes without saying that I love it even more for dinner!

But as life has sped up and become busier and more hectic and frantic the first thing in the morning, having a make-ahead breakfast on hand has become key. And if I don't have something made ahead of time, I at least like to have a plan. One that is preferably easy, simple, nourishing, satisfying, and let's be real, one that can be made in mere minutes.

Here's the thing though: I also love a slow, lounging-style morning. One where the kitchen smells like coffee for hours, smooth jazz is playing through the speakers, and breakfast is served around the table without the hustle and bustle of life hanging over our heads.

Because of that, you'll find two different kinds of recipes here in this chapter. Some can be made ahead of time. They are the ones that you prepare for yourself the night before, the ones that make you excited to go to bed because you *just can't wait* to get up and eat. Recipes such as Peanut Butter Chocolate Oatmeal Cups (page 61), mousse-like Vanilla Bean Chia Seed Pudding (page 76), and my Fluffy Make-Ahead Egg Bites (page 66) that are like mini soufflé cups.

And then there are those that are still easy, but you make them when you have a bit more time. Think puff pastry quiche (page 69; no fussy pie dough here!), Crispy Baked Breakfast Quesadillas with Pico de Gallo (page 55; the cheese is so melty), and Strawberries & Cream Steel-Cut Oats (page 56).

Oh, and just wait until you try my Iced Blueberry Lattes (page 78). It is a coffee dream!

P.S. When it comes to my 10-minute meal prep strategy, you will find that for breakfast, a lot of the time this means measuring out ingredients and storing them until you're ready to make the recipe. Don't underestimate how great of a tip this is, despite it seeming trivial! It truly saves a good 10 to 15 minutes for each recipe, and when it comes to mealtime, that is huge. ●

whipped cottage cheese protein pancakes

1½ cups cottage cheese

3 large eggs

1 cup rolled oats

1 tablespoon baking powder

1 tablespoon maple syrup, plus extra for serving

½ teaspoon kosher salt

½ teaspoon cinnamon

2 teaspoons pure vanilla extract

Butter, for cooking the pancakes

Chopped fruit, for serving (optional)

Confectioners' sugar, for serving (optional)

I am so glad that cottage cheese is having a moment. Because up until now, it has been the Brussels sprouts of breakfast. Especially for me.

For most of my life, I loathed cottage cheese. Or at least, I thought I did. It turns out that I was just consuming it the wrong way. When I was a kid, the only way people ate cottage cheese was in a bowl with syrupy peaches or pineapple. I am so glad we have evolved. These days, my favorite way to consume cottage cheese is in a savory manner. You know—thinking of it as a savory cheese!

However, the versatility of this ingredient can't be overlooked. The satiety factor is incredible, thanks to the protein. And the ways that it can be used, whether it's scooped, spread, or whipped, makes it one of the most-used ingredients in my kitchen!

These fluffy, fabulous pancakes are my favorite way to use cottage cheese for breakfast in a sweet way. They can be drizzled with syrup and saucy blueberries or can even be served with an egg and my pepita crunch (page 45) on top. The result is a filling, satisfying pancake that will hold you over until lunch!

Add the cottage cheese, eggs, oats, baking powder, maple syrup, salt, cinnamon, and vanilla to a blender and puree until smooth.

Heat a skillet or grill over medium-low heat. Once hot, add a dollop of butter and spread it all over the pan.

Add the pancake batter to the pan using a ¼-cup measure. Allow 1 to 2 inches between the pancakes for easy flipping. Cook until bubbles appear on the top of the batter, then gently flip and cook for 2 to 3 minutes more, until the pancakes are fully set.

Transfer the pancakes to a plate and repeat with the remaining batter. Serve the pancakes with maple syrup, fruit, or even confectioners' sugar, if desired. These are delicious warm or even chilled straight from the fridge!

10-Minute Meal Prep

These pancakes can be prepared fully ahead of time and stored in the fridge (3 days) or freezer (3 months!). Simply reheat and serve.

easy everyday

crispy baked breakfast quesadillas with pico de gallo

½ tablespoon unsalted butter

4 large eggs

Kosher salt and black pepper

1 tablespoon extra-virgin olive oil

4 large burrito-size flour tortillas

¾ cup freshly grated Cheddar cheese

¾ cup black beans

Sour cream, for serving

pico de gallo

1 pint cherry tomatoes, quartered

½ medium sweet onion, diced

¼ cup cilantro, chopped, plus more for serving

½ lime, juiced

Kosher salt and black pepper

10-Minute Meal Prep

The pico de gallo can be made 1 day ahead of time. Pre-portion out all the ingredients and store them in the fridge for easy grab-and-go making. You can also reheat leftover quesadillas each morning; they will just not be quite as crisp. They last for 2 to 3 days in the fridge. Still delicious!

I grew up in the microwaved-quesadilla era: Throw some shredded cheese from a bag on a flour tortilla, fold it up, and microwave until melty. And while my very nostalgic, cheese-loving self still finds this to be a delicious concept at times, I can never go back from a crispy, baked quesadilla. As long as I have the time!

This is such an easy method for making a whole batch of quesadillas at once. There is no microwaving one at a time or frying one at a time in a pan. Baking the quesadillas means that you can make multiples—maybe two or four, depending on tortilla size—at once!

I've used this method for years on taco night and am happy to say that it works wonders for breakfast, too. Scramble some eggs, add your other favorite toppings, and you're good to go. The key is brushing or spraying the pan with olive oil, so every square inch of the tortilla gets deliciously golden, toasty, and crispy. Grab a breakfast triangle and you're on your way!

Preheat the oven to 425°F.

Melt the butter in a nonstick pan over medium-low heat.

In a bowl, mix the eggs with a big pinch of salt and pepper. Pour them in the pan and cook, gently pushing in the sides and scrambling the eggs until just firm, about 2 to 3 minutes. Turn off the heat.

Brush a baking sheet with ½ tablespoon of the olive oil. Lay two tortillas on the baking sheet. Divide the eggs between the tortillas, then top each with the Cheddar and black beans. Place the other two tortillas on top, creating a quesadilla. Brush the tops of each quesadilla with the remaining ½ tablespoon of olive oil.

Put the baking sheet in the oven and bake for 8 minutes. Remove the sheet from the oven and, using two spatulas, gently flip the quesadillas to crisp up the other side. Return the sheet to the oven and bake for about 5 minutes more.

While the quesadillas are baking, make the pico de gallo: Combine the tomatoes, onion, cilantro, lime juice, and a pinch of salt and pepper in a bowl. Stir.

Let the quesadillas cool slightly. Slice them into four triangles, then top with the pico and sour cream.

strawberries & cream steel-cut oats

strawberry sauce

1 cup chopped strawberries

2 tablespoons sugar

oats

2 tablespoons unsalted butter

1 cup steel-cut oats

¼ teaspoon cinnamon, plus extra for serving

2 cups water

1½ cups canned coconut milk, plus more for serving

½ teaspoon kosher salt

2 teaspoons pure vanilla extract

Honey or maple syrup (optional)

Sliced strawberries, for serving

Freeze-dried strawberries, crushed, for serving (optional)

Seeds or nuts of your choice, for serving (optional)

10-Minute Meal Prep

The strawberry sauce can be made ahead of time and stored in the fridge for 2 to 3 days. Measure out all the ingredients and chop the strawberries ahead of time, keeping them stored in the fridge, too. When ready to make, grab everything and go!

I always thought my heart would belong to instant oatmeal, preferably the strawberries-and-cream version. This was an ultimate comfort food for me growing up and waking up to a warm bowl of it in my tween years set me off for the day on the right foot.

Then I learned how to make it on my own. The grown-up version. The almost-gourmet version! The version that leaves me feeling extra nourished, full and satisfied, while giving me an incredible creamy texture that instant oats just don't provide.

Steel-cut oats will always be my favorite, mostly because I am a texture freak. I love anything with chew and/or crunch, and steel-cut oats provide that. The only downside is that they require a longer cook time and a good bit of stirring. So, this is a recipe I love to make when I have more time on my hands.

However, you can also make a batch of this ahead of time! Prepare it on the weekend for the busy mornings ahead. I reheat portions of it in a saucepan, adding more water or milk as needed until that creamy consistency returns.

Tastes like heaven.

make the strawberry sauce Combine the strawberries and sugar in a saucepan over medium heat. Cook, stirring often, until the berries soften and break down, 6 to 8 minutes, releasing juice and creating a sauce. Cook for another 10 to 12 minutes, until the sauce is bubbling. Remove from the heat.

make the oats Melt the butter in a pot or large skillet over medium-low heat. Stir in the oats and cinnamon. Cook, stirring often, until the oats are toasty, 3 to 4 minutes.

Pour in the water, coconut milk, and salt. Bring the mixture to a boil, then reduce it to a simmer. Cook, stirring often, for about 15 minutes, until most of the liquid is absorbed. Stir in the strawberry sauce and vanilla. Taste and, if needed, add a bit of honey, if desired, to sweeten.

Serve with fresh strawberries or crushed freeze-dried strawberries on top, as well as a sprinkle of seeds or nuts, if desired.

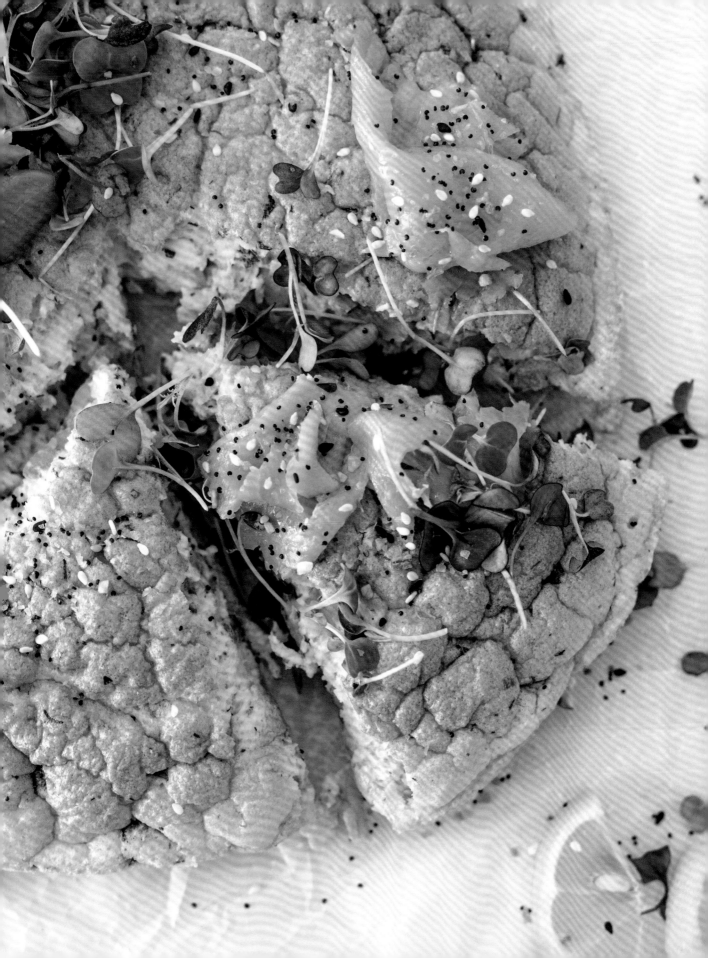

everything smoked salmon frittata soufflé

8 large eggs, separated

4 scallions, thinly sliced

2 garlic cloves, minced

2 tablespoons chopped fresh parsley, plus more for serving

2 tablespoons chopped fresh dill, plus more for serving

2 tablespoons capers

4 ounces goat cheese, crumbled

1 tablespoon everything bagel seasoning, plus more for serving

8 ounces smoked salmon, torn into pieces

2 tablespoons unsalted butter

Microgreens, for serving

I am always looking for ways to incorporate smoked salmon into my meals. It's one of my favorite foods, plus it is so easy to use. While smoked salmon mostly finds its way into our home during holiday seasons or when we host a brunch or have guests over, occasionally I will grab it just so we can enjoy it and make the day feel fancy and special.

Aside from piling it high on a bagel or toast, I love using it in a frittata. The flavor is incredible, it's a simple way to elevate those eggs, and the everything bagel seasoning makes it taste like one giant breakfast bagel.

Serve it with some toasted sourdough and you've got the perfect breakfast on hand!

Preheat the oven to 375°F.

Place the egg whites in the bowl of a stand mixer. Place the egg yolks in a large mixing bowl.

To the egg yolks, add the scallions, garlic, parsley, dill, capers, goat cheese, and everything bagel seasoning. Whisk until combined. Stir in the smoked salmon pieces.

Beat the egg whites in the mixer at medium-high speed until medium peaks form, 4 to 5 minutes. Fold the egg whites into the egg yolk mixture. Do not whisk the mixture—fold it until completely combined and fluffy.

Melt the butter in a 10-inch skillet over medium-low heat. As soon as the butter starts to get brown bits on the bottom, pour in the frittata mixture. Use a spatula to smooth out the top. Cook for about 5 minutes, until the eggs just start to set, then turn off the heat.

Stick the pan in the oven. Bake the frittata for 15 to 18 minutes, until golden brown and puffed. Make sure the center is cooked through.

Top with parsley and dill, more everything bagel seasoning, and some microgreens before serving.

10-Minute Meal Prep

Measure out all the ingredients ahead of time and keep them stored in the fridge until ready to make.

peanut butter chocolate oatmeal cups

2½ cups old-fashioned rolled oats

1 teaspoon baking powder

1 teaspoon cinnamon

½ teaspoon kosher salt

1 large egg

1¼ cups milk

3 tablespoons maple syrup or honey

2 teaspoons pure vanilla extract

½ cup creamy peanut butter, melted

½ cup chocolate chips of your choice, melted

You already know about my love of oatmeal. The chew, the way it's so completely satisfying, not to mention the brain power I feel that I get from having an excellent, nourishing breakfast. Which is why I try just about any and all flavor combinations when it comes to oats. And peanut butter + chocolate tops my list. It always has!

These oatmeal cups are the perfect breakfast or snack to prepare ahead of time. Make a batch on the weekend, then store them in the fridge. They can be reheated and served warm (and melty with chocolate, oh my) or even chilled (I love them this way). They are such a great grab-and-go option, and they make enough that you have a few days' worth.

You can also experiment with different nut butters, fruits, seeds, and toppings to this recipe. It's pretty forgiving and a fun one to play with!

Preheat the oven to 350°F. Spray a twelve-cup muffin tin with nonstick baking spray.

In a small bowl, whisk together the oats, baking powder, cinnamon, and salt.

In a large bowl, whisk together the egg, milk, maple syrup, and vanilla. Whisk in the melted peanut butter.

Stir the dry ingredients into the wet ingredients until just combined. Divide the mixture evenly among the twelve muffin cups.

Bake for about 25 minutes, until set and golden.

While the muffins are cooling, melt the chocolate chips. Place them in a microwave-safe bowl and microwave at 50% power for 30 seconds, stirring after each increment. Continue to microwave and stir until the chocolate is fully melted—this may take three or four intervals. When the muffins are done, drizzle with the melted chocolate. Let the chocolate set for 5 minutes, then serve!

10-Minute Meal Prep

Measure out all the wet and dry ingredients ahead of time, storing them in the fridge. Store the finished cups in the fridge in a sealed container for up to 5 days.

salted chocolate coconut granola bark

3 cups old-fashioned rolled oats

1¼ cups unsweetened shredded coconut

1 cup whole almonds, chopped

½ cup almond flour

¼ cup ground flaxseed

¼ cup chia seeds

¼ cup hemp hearts

½ cup maple syrup

½ cup brown sugar

¼ cup water

3 teaspoons pure vanilla extract

1 teaspoon pumpkin spice

1 teaspoon kosher salt

⅓ cup avocado, canola, or vegetable oil

1 large egg white, whisked until frothy

chocolate topping

1 cup dark chocolate chips, melted

1 tablespoon coconut oil

¼ cup flaked coconut

1 teaspoon flaky salt

10-Minute Meal Prep

Measure out all the ingredients ahead of time before making.

Let's be real here: Granola bark is simply granola that is broken into big shards, instead of tiny crumbles.

Granola bark is perfect for grabbing as you run out the door or for munching on as an afternoon snack. It's great when crumbled into yogurt or oatmeal and also makes for a nice cheese board addition. I like to use it on a snack plate: A few berries, some slices of cheese, and a shard of granola bark is satisfying and holds me over until my next meal. The salty-sweet combo you get here will forever be a favorite of mine.

Preheat the oven to 325°F. Line a 13 × 18-inch baking sheet with parchment paper.

In a large bowl, stir together the oats, coconut, almonds, almond flour, flaxseed, chia seeds, and hemp hearts.

In a medium saucepan, combine the maple syrup, brown sugar, and water together in a saucepan. Bring to a simmer and whisk until the sugar has dissolved, 1 to 2 minutes. Remove the pan from the heat and whisk in the vanilla, pumpkin spice, and salt. Whisk in the oil and egg white until combined. Let cool for 5 to 10 minutes.

Once cool, pour the mixture into the dry ingredients. Stir to combine and make sure all the oats, seeds, and nuts are evenly mixed with the liquid.

Press the mixture into the pan, making sure it's in one even layer. You can use another baking sheet to press down on the granola to make sure it's packed tightly into the sheet.

Bake for 40 to 45 minutes, rotating the sheet twice during cook time, until the granola is deeply golden and brown. Let cool completely.

Remove the sheet from the oven. Place the chocolate and coconut oil in a microwave-safe bowl. Microwave on 50% power for 30 seconds, stirring after each increment. This will take 2 to 3 minutes total. Pour it over the granola bark and spread it evenly to cover the top. Sprinkle with the coconut and flaky salt.

Let the granola bark set before breaking it into pieces. Store it in a sealed container for up to 1 week.

banana zucchini muffins

1½ cups all-purpose flour

¾ cups old-fashioned rolled oats

1 teaspoon baking soda

½ teaspoon baking powder

½ teaspoon cinnamon

½ teaspoon kosher salt

2 large eggs

½ cup granulated sugar

½ cup brown sugar

½ cup canola or other neutral oil,
or coconut oil

2 teaspoons pure vanilla extract

1 cup mashed bananas (about
2 large or 3 medium bananas)

1 cup grated zucchini

1 cup chocolate chips of your choice
(optional)

I'm telling you about these muffins in the breakfast chapter, but do you know when I really love to eat them? At night. Right before bed. Or as a post-dinner snack!

That is when my kids love to have a muffin like this, too. Filled with fruit and vegetables, these are like a little cake bite that satisfies our sweet tooth while filling us up ahead of a good night's sleep.

Of course, you can also make a batch and serve them for breakfast. Muffins are perfect any time of day!

Preheat the oven to 375°F. Line a twelve-cup muffin tin with liners.

Whisk together the flour, oats, baking soda, baking powder, cinnamon, and salt in a medium bowl.

In a large bowl, whisk together the eggs and sugars until combined. Whisk in the oil and vanilla until combined. Mix in the mashed bananas, then the zucchini.

Using a mixing spoon, stir the dry ingredients into the wet ingredients until just combined—do not overmix. Stir in the chocolate chips, if desired.

Fill the muffin cups about three-quarters of the way full. Bake the muffins for 18 to 20 minutes, or until set in the center. Let cool before serving!

Store in a sealed container for 4 to 5 days. The muffins can also be frozen for up to 3 months.

10-Minute Meal Prep

Measure out all the ingredients ahead of time and store them in the fridge.

fluffy make-ahead egg bites

8 large eggs, separated

2 garlic cloves, minced

½ cup freshly grated fontina cheese

2 tablespoons chopped chives

Kosher salt and black pepper

2 tablespoons unsalted butter

These make-ahead egg bites may look a tad boring, but trust me, they are the perfect base for adding in **anything you want**. Truly, almost anything!

I keep the base of these little soufflés simple: salt and pepper, herbs, maybe a sprinkling of cheese. But you can add in so much: chopped peppers or tomatoes, sautéed spinach, or even chopped cooked sausage.

I love making these on the weekend and sticking them in the fridge. Much like my oatmeal cups (page 61), they are great for grab-and-go breakfast and snacks. And they are also really delish eaten cold, at room temperature, or after a 15-second zap in the microwave.

These will never look super pretty, but they are super delicious. I love having these on hand when we have mornings that include getting everyone ready quickly, rushing out of the house, and trying not to forget anything. Knowing that I have a protein-packed bite for all of us to eat keeps me at ease.

And just so you know, my kids love to slice these in half and dip them in ketchup! Almost like an egg nugget. I won't tell if you won't.

Preheat the oven to 375°F. Spray a twelve-cup muffin tin with nonstick spray.

Place the egg whites in the bowl of a stand mixer. Place the egg yolks in a large mixing bowl.

To the egg yolks, add the garlic, fontina, chives, and a big pinch of salt and pepper. Whisk until combined.

Beat the egg whites in the mixer at medium-high speed until medium peaks form, 4 to 5 minutes. Fold the egg whites into the egg yolk mixture. Do not whisk the mixture—fold it until completely combined and fluffy.

Divide the egg mixture evenly among the muffin cups.

Bake the bites for 15 to 18 minutes, until golden brown and puffed. Make sure the center is cooked through and not jiggling.

These will be super puffy at first and will fall as they sit. Store in the fridge for 3 to 4 days for quick-and-easy breakfasts!

10-Minute Meal Prep

You can prepare the ingredients the day before. Grate the cheese, measure out the other ingredients, including separating the eggs, and store in the fridge until ready to make.

the easiest fancy puff pastry quiche

6 slices bacon, chopped

1 pound asparagus, cut into thirds

Kosher salt and black pepper

1 sheet puff pastry, thawed if frozen

8 large eggs

1½ cups heavy cream

½ cup freshly grated white Cheddar cheese

½ cup freshly grated Gruyère cheese

3 garlic cloves, minced

¼ cup chopped fresh herbs, like parsley, thyme and chives, plus more for serving

Note: For best results, I like to use puff pastry that comes in one single sheet. You can usually find these in the refrigerated section of your grocery store with prepared piecrusts.

10-Minute Meal Prep

The bacon and asparagus can be cooked ahead of time and stored in the fridge. You can also measure out all the ingredients 1 to 2 days ahead of time before making.

Puff pastry is an ingredient that I always have in my fridge and use in the kitchen constantly. Whether it's for breakfast, lunch, or dinner, I can always find a way to use puff pastry. And as someone who has always struck out with classic piecrust, it saves me every single time.

Using puff pastry to make a big sheet-pan quiche is one of my favorite uses. It's a fabulous way to serve a crowd and it looks so impressive. Not to mention that it tastes incredible, with its flaky, buttery layers. It is almost like using a croissant crust in your quiche, and no one can complain about that!

Another use for this recipe is to make it ahead of time for pre-portioned breakfasts throughout the week. Sure, puff pastry never tastes quite as good as when it just comes out of the oven, and it will lose a bit of the flaky crispness. But I still give the leftovers a solid A-.

I'll make a pan of this, slice it into squares for Eddie and me for dinner, then reheat a few in the morning. It is so incredibly satisfying. And it's pretty, too!

Preheat the oven to 425°F.

Heat a skillet over medium-low heat and add the bacon. Cook, stirring often, until the fat is rendered and the bacon is crispy, 6 to 8 minutes. Remove the bacon with a slotted spoon and place it on a paper towel to drain the excess grease.

Add the asparagus to the same skillet with a pinch of salt and pepper. Cook for about 5 minutes, just to soften it slightly. Remove it with the slotted spoon and place it on the paper towel with the bacon.

Lay the puff pastry in a 9 × 13-inch sheet pan. The pastry may go up the sides of the pan a bit. Poke it all over with a fork; this helps to keep it from bubbling up.

Whisk together the eggs, cream, cheeses, garlic, and herbs until combined. Stir in a pinch of salt and pepper. Stir in the bacon and the asparagus.

Pour the egg mixture into the puff pastry crust.

Bake for 25 to 30 minutes, until the center is no longer jiggly and the crust is golden. Remove and let cool slightly. Sprinkle with the additional herbs. Slice into eight squares to serve. This lasts in the fridge for 2 to 3 days.

rosemary bacon skillet sweet potatoes

6 slices bacon

4 sweet potatoes, peeled and chopped into 1-inch cubes

Kosher salt and black pepper

3 tablespoons chopped fresh rosemary

Never underestimate the power of a crispy breakfast potato. Especially one made with crispy bacon and sizzled rosemary. *Especially* when that potato is sweet. Sweet, savory, crunchy, herby. This recipe checks all the breakfast boxes.

It's one that I make often for dinner, too. It's excellent as a side to fried or scrambled eggs, but also perfect if you want something to go with roasted chicken or fish.

No one ever complains when they see these little crispy bites on the table. You should probably make a double batch and freeze some for later!

Heat a large cast-iron skillet over medium-low heat and add the bacon. Cook, stirring often, until the fat is rendered and the bacon is crispy, 6 to 8 minutes. Remove the bacon with a slotted spoon and place it on a paper towel to drain any excess grease.

Increase the heat to medium. Add the sweet potatoes to the skillet with a big pinch of salt and pepper. Toss them to coat in the bacon fat, then arrange them in a (mostly) single layer. Cook for about 8 minutes, letting the bottoms get golden and crisp, before tossing and cooking on another side. Cook for another 8 to 10 minutes, then flip again. Repeat this until the potatoes are deeply golden and tender.

Stir the rosemary into the skillet a few minutes before the potatoes are done. Stir in the bacon and serve! These last in the fridge for 2 to 3 days.

10-Minute Meal Prep

Chop the bacon ahead of time and store it in a container in the fridge. Chop the rosemary, too, and store it in the fridge until ready to use. Peel and chop the sweet potatoes 12 to 24 hours beforehand, storing them in ice water in the fridge.

crispy rice with fried eggs

1 tablespoon extra-virgin olive oil

1 cup cooked jasmine rice, preferably leftover

2 scallions, thinly sliced

Kosher salt and black pepper

¼ cup freshly grated sharp Cheddar cheese

2 eggs, fried, poached, or soft boiled

Chili oil, for serving (optional)

Have leftover rice? Crisp it up and serve it with a fried or poached egg. I swear, this will become one of your favorite breakfasts.

Because we are side dish lovers over here, I almost always make too much rice with dinner. These days, I do it accidentally on purpose, just so I can make this for breakfast.

Crisping the rice in the skillet gives it an incredible texture. It's one that I crave and love, making this the ultimate comfort food for me. It's fantastic as breakfast, but also makes for a great quick dinner. Especially on nights I'm home alone—I curl up with a bowl of this and it feels like meal paradise. Try it!

Heat the olive oil in a large skillet over medium heat. In a medium bowl, stir together the rice, most of the scallions, and a pinch of salt and pepper.

Press the rice into a single layer in the skillet. Cook until the rice is golden and crispy, 5 to 6 minutes. Sprinkle with the Cheddar cheese. This is the time when I cook my eggs, too!

Use a spatula to gently flip the rice and press the cheesy side into the skillet. Cook for a few more minutes, until it gets golden and toasty.

Spoon the rice into two bowls. Top each with an egg—whether it's fried, poached, or even soft boiled. Top with the remaining scallions and a sprinkle of salt and pepper. Drizzle on some chili oil if you'd like. Serve!

10-Minute Meal Prep

If you don't already have leftover rice, make a batch and store it in the fridge just to make this recipe!

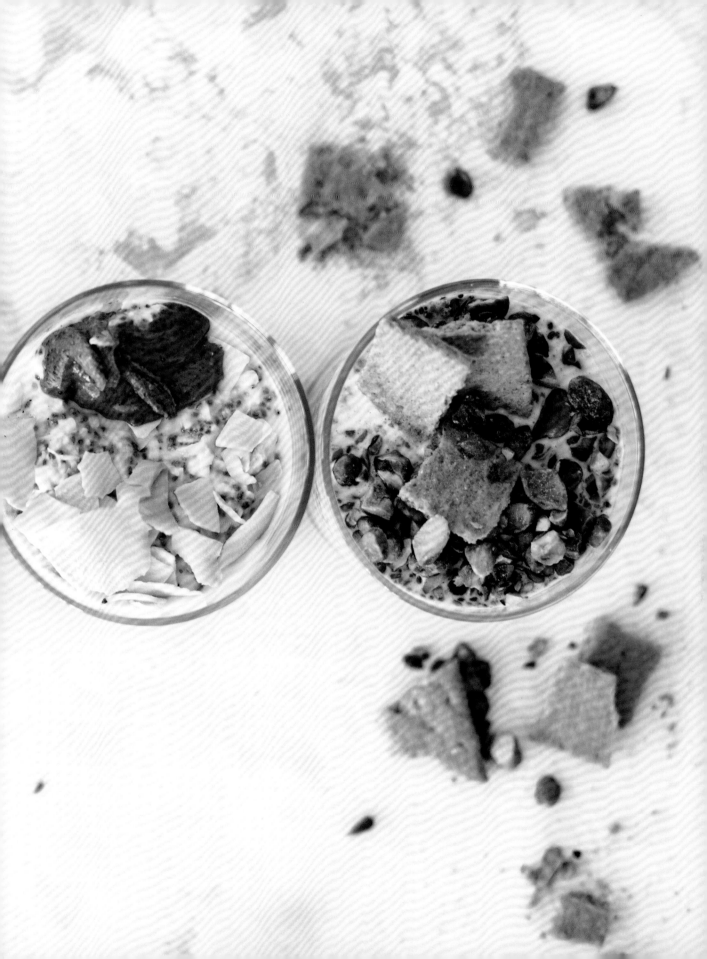

vanilla bean chia seed pudding, 4 ways

2 cups milk (any variety works!)

½ cup chia seeds

1 tablespoon honey

1 tablespoon vanilla bean paste

2 teaspoons pure vanilla extract

¼ teaspoon kosher salt

Chopped fruit, granola, nuts, and/or honey, for serving

Chia seed pudding has been a staple in my breakfast routine for more than a decade. Now, my kids love it, too. They think of it as breakfast dessert, and they aren't wrong. Even just a hint of sweet berries, maybe a sprinkling of dark chocolate, a drizzle of honey—heck, even a shake of rainbow sprinkles—make this taste like actual pudding. Sometimes we even eat it as dessert!

My tip for chia pudding is to prepare enough for two or three days at a time. I make it in a large bowl, then portion it out into jars or glasses and stick it in the fridge to set. Anyone who wants one can grab it from the fridge.

I've made so many variations of this over the years, but these four flavors are the ones I come back to the most. The chai is spiced and warm. The raspberry dark chocolate is fruity and rich. The almond butter coconut is creamy and tropical. And the pistachio pie is buttery and nutty with a hint of crunchy graham cracker. I don't know which one I love the most!

Combine the milk, chia seeds, honey, vanilla paste and extract, and salt in a large bowl and mix. Divide the mixture evenly among four jars. I like to use a 6- or 8-ounce jar for these.

Cover and place in the fridge for at least 4 hours, or overnight. When ready to eat, serve with fruit, granola, nuts, honey, and more. These keep in the fridge for 3 to 4 days.

chai chia pudding

1 teaspoon cinnamon, plus extra for serving

½ teaspoon cardamom

¼ teaspoon ground cloves

¼ teaspoon ground ginger

Star anise or cinnamon stick, for garnish

Stir the ground cinnamon, cardamom, cloves, and ginger into the milk and chia mixture. Cover and place in the fridge for at least 4 hours, or overnight. Top with a sprinkling of cinnamon and either a star anise or cinnamon stick.

dark chocolate raspberry chia pudding

⅓ cup cocoa powder

¼ cup crushed freeze-dried raspberries, plus extra for serving

1 cup fresh raspberries

Coconut cream, for serving

Stir the cocoa powder and freeze-dried raspberries into the chia pudding mixture. Cover and place in the fridge for at least 4 hours, or overnight. When ready to serve, top with the fresh raspberries, a dollop of coconut cream, and a sprinkling of crushed freeze-dried raspberries.

almond butter coconut chia pudding

⅓ cup unsweetened shredded coconut

¼ teaspoon coconut extract

½ cup almond butter

½ cup toasted coconut flakes

Stir the shredded coconut and coconut extract into the chia and milk mixture. Put 2 tablespoons of almond butter at the bottom of each jar before dividing the chia pudding. Cover and place in the fridge for at least 4 hours, or overnight. When ready to serve, sprinkle with the toasted coconut flakes.

pistachio pie chia pudding

2 cups coconut milk

1 tablespoon graham cracker crumbs, plus extra for serving

¼ teaspoon almond extract

2 tablespoons chopped pistachios

In place of the milk in the vanilla bean chia pudding recipe, use the coconut milk as the base for your chia pudding. Stir in the graham cracker crumbs and almond extract when mixing. When the pudding is set, top with the chopped pistachios and a sprinkle of graham cracker crumbs.

10-Minute Meal Prep

Chia pudding is the ultimate prep-ahead recipe! This entire thing will only take you 10 minutes to prepare! Make it the night before and enjoy it for breakfast or make it in the early morning for an after-dinner snack.

iced blueberry lattes

blueberry sauce

1 cup blueberries

¼ cup sugar

½ lemon, juiced

lattes

4 tablespoons blueberry sauce,
or more to taste

2 shots espresso

1 cup milk, or more to taste

I have always been a cold coffee lover. Pour my caffeine over ice and I am here. for. it.

The coldness makes your coffee smoother, and I've always thought it resembles ice cream. It reminds me of the coffee ice cream that my grandparents always had in their freezer, and that is a memory I will gladly keep refreshing.

I was skeptical of the berry + coffee combo until I had an iced berry latte on vacation a few years ago. My mind was BLOWN. The berry flavor just *worked* with the nutty, rich coffee beans. And it's one that I love whether the coffee is black or there's a nice cream cloud poured into the glass.

Add a spoonful to your glass when you make an iced latte and you're instantly transported somewhere warm and summery. Which is such a wonderful thing.

And, I mean, just look at this color. Stunning!

make the blueberry sauce Combine the berries, sugar, and lemon juice in a saucepan over medium heat. Cook, stirring often, until the blueberries burst and begin to get saucy, 6 to 8 minutes. I use a wooden spoon to smash them if needed. Simmer for 8 to 10 minutes, until thickened like syrup, then remove from the heat. Pour the mixture into a jar and let it cool completely before using. Store in the fridge for up to 1 week; this will make more blueberry sauce than needed for two drinks. If you won't finish it in a week, you can freeze the remaining sauce for up to 3 months.

make the lattes Fill two glasses with crushed ice. Add 2 tablespoons of the blueberry sauce and a shot of espresso to each glass. Serve with ½ cup of milk each. Taste and add more sauce or milk as desired!

10-Minute Meal Prep

Make the blueberry sauce ahead of time and keep it stored in the fridge.

CHAPTER 3

lunch loves

It goes without saying that I love to cook. I live to be in the kitchen. After all, I'm rambling on and on to you in a cookbook about all my favorite foods.

But there is one thing I don't love, and that is cooking every single meal, every single day. Frankly, I don't want to cook breakfast, lunch, and dinner in the same day.

And maybe it's not even about the actual cooking part. It's more about the cleaning up. Right? I definitely don't want to cook lunch, clean up, and then start cooking dinner a few hours later, just to have to clean up again. And again. Life is all about cleaning up the kitchen, every single day. I like to minimize a bit of that, thank you very much.

For that reason, most of my lunches consist of things I can make ahead of time. This means I can grab them straight from the fridge and eat. Because this meal also happens to fall during work hours (how rude!), I don't want to spend any extra time cooking and cleaning.

Now, of course, there is an exception. Many of the lunches I love the most do incorporate an ingredient that has to be cooked or takes some time to prepare. It's not just PB&J over here, every day.

Because of that, I like to choose recipes that stretch themselves. Ones that require one day of cooking, meaning I might prepare three of those lunches on a Sunday or Monday. This usually consists of cooking grains, roasting vegetables, or whisking together a sauce ahead of time.

Almost every meal in this chapter is incredible when it's prepared beforehand. Which means many of these are also portable—you can take them on the go, to work or on a picnic or to a friend's house.

Who doesn't love that?! ●

pomegranate kale slaw salad

1 medium head of green cabbage, thinly sliced

4 cups curly or Tuscan kale, thinly sliced

2 pears, cut into matchsticks

1 large shallot or ½ small red onion, thinly sliced

¾ cup shredded carrots

½ cup pomegranate arils

Kosher salt and black pepper

⅓ cup roasted pepitas

⅓ cup toasted walnuts or pecans, chopped

1 batch Citrus Vinaigrette (page 33)

Is it a slaw? Or a salad? It's basically both! This crunchy and refreshing slaw salad is filled with thinly sliced cabbage, pears, kale, and more. This recipe is so versatile that you won't even know where to begin!

It's lovely on its own, or use it as a side dish for dinner, as a light little lunch, or take it to a potluck as a main dish that people can pile on their plates with everything else. It's an excellent base salad. Use it to layer on grilled chicken, shrimp, roasted chickpeas, and more.

The slaw factor is also incredible. Mix it up and serve it in sandwiches, on saucy pulled pork, barbecued chicken, or even tuna on toast. Tacos, too!

Slaw salads are the new chopped salads. Tiny shreds of ingredients make everything crunchy and crisp and fun to eat. It's also a beautiful dish for the holiday season. Peep those pomegranate jewels!

In a large bowl, combine the cabbage, kale, pears, shallots, carrots, and pomegranate. Sprinkle with a pinch of salt and pepper and toss well. Add the pepitas and nuts. Drizzle with a few tablespoons of the dressing and toss. Let the slaw sit for 5 to 10 minutes before serving.

You can assemble the ingredients ahead of time; just wait to dress it until a few minutes before serving. Because the slaw is made with kale, it lasts a bit longer in the fridge than traditional slaw. I find that it keeps well for 1 to 2 days.

10-Minute Meal Prep

The dressing can be made ahead of time. The kale can also be chopped ahead of time and stored in a resealable bag with a paper towel. The nuts can also be chopped ahead of time.

white bean tuna orzo

1 cup dry orzo

1 tablespoon red wine vinegar

1 teaspoon Dijon mustard

2 garlic cloves, minced or grated

⅓ cup chopped roasted red peppers, plus 1 tablespoon oil from the jar

¼ cup extra-virgin olive oil

Kosher salt and black pepper

1 (14-ounce) can cannellini beans, drained and rinsed

1 (5-ounce) can tuna packed in water, drained

⅓ cup chopped fresh herbs, like dill, parsley, and/or chives

¼ cup Quick Pickled Onions (page 40)

This might be my most-made make-ahead lunch salad. It can be found on repeat almost every other week, and it's incredibly satisfying and delicious.

I ate a lot of tuna growing up. My mom was the queen of tuna sandwiches and I loved them. These days, I still love tuna but am always looking for other ways to enjoy it. Serving it in a different way has been a game changer for my kids, too. We all go crazy over this orzo!

One of the best parts about this recipe is that you can make a very large portion and it will last. This is a fantastic straight-from-the-fridge meal and it stays good for days. I'll either keep it in a large bowl or portion it out, and I serve it a few different ways, too. I like this as a salad topping, piled high on a bed of greens. And sometimes I scoop it into lettuce cups or wraps, which adds an additional refreshing crunch.

Satiating and simple. Gotta love that.

Cook the orzo according to the package directions. Once finished, transfer the orzo to a large bowl.

Whisk together the vinegar, mustard, garlic, the oil from the roasted red peppers, the olive oil, and a big pinch of salt and pepper.

Drizzle half of the dressing over the orzo. Add the beans, tuna, roasted red peppers, herbs, and pickled onions and mix together. Drizzle with the remaining dressing and serve. This stays good in the fridge for 3 to 4 days.

10-Minute Meal Prep

The orzo can be cooked ahead of time and stored in the fridge. The dressing can also be made beforehand and kept in the fridge. The beans can be rinsed ahead of time and the peppers can be chopped, too.

honey mustard broccoli quinoa salad

1 pound broccoli florets

2 tablespoons extra-virgin olive oil

Kosher salt and black pepper

1 cup dry quinoa

1 (14-ounce) can chickpeas, drained and rinsed

⅓ cup roasted, salted pepitas

⅓ cup dried cranberries

1 batch Honey Mustard Vinaigrette (page 31)

Let me tell you a lunch prep secret: Many days, I prepare lunch while making dinner. YES.

It is a total game changer when it comes to time-saving meal prep. Especially when said lunch includes a lot of ingredients that I'd usually use for dinner. Or in this case, I make simple ingredients that take just a little time to cook (like simmering grains and roasting vegetables). I do it at dinnertime, while I'm already cooking other things. This has been one of the biggest things that has saved me time and frustration over the years, while keeping hungry mouths fed.

This quinoa salad is the perfect way to test that method. All the ingredients in this salad require preparation, which normally is annoying. But the prep is simple and easy, along with being fairly quick. It's just that I don't want to boil quinoa, roast broccoli, *and* whisk up a dressing all during weekday lunchtime. You know?

So, during dinner the night before, I'll set a pot of quinoa to boil. I'll also roast broccoli—and that may be as simple as adding some extra broccoli to the sheet pan that I'm already making for dinner. (We love broccoli around here. My inner ten-year-old is shocked while simultaneously thrilled.)

The dressing comes together in mere minutes, but taking out all those bottles and ingredients for the dressing adds time. So, I'll either whisk it up on the weekend or make it during dinner. It's so easy and I'm already standing in the kitchen, cleaning things up.

Now, you get a tasty sweet, savory, and satisfying lunch bowl out of that hard work. Enjoy!

Preheat the oven to 425°F. Toss the broccoli with the olive oil and a big pinch of salt and pepper.

Roast the broccoli on a sheet pan for about 20 minutes, until golden and tender.

While the broccoli roasts, make the quinoa according to the package directions. It should take about 15 minutes.

When the quinoa and broccoli are finished, combine both in a large bowl. Stir in a few tablespoons of the dressing. Stir in the chickpeas, pepitas, and dried cranberries. Toss a few more times to combine. Enjoy! This stays great in the fridge for 2 to 3 days.

10-Minute Meal Prep

The quinoa and dressing can be made ahead of time. The broccoli can be roasted ahead of time! Keep them all in the fridge until ready to use.

tortellini caprese salad

16 ounces cheese tortellini

5 ounces baby arugula

Kosher salt and black pepper

2 cups cherry tomatoes, chopped

1 cup fresh mozzarella cheese balls (bocconcini)

½ cup chopped fresh basil

1 batch I Adore This Balsamic Dressing (page 31)

Cheese tortellini is the way to my heart. The tender little packages of cheese-filled pasta, plump and savory, work in so many ways. I love adding them to soups and salads, and the best part is that most tortellini cooks in less than 5 minutes and can be prepped ahead of time.

Next to orzo, tortellini is my favorite pasta to use in a cold fridge salad. It can be tossed with greens and a vinaigrette. It's incredibly satisfying and very kid-friendly. Not only do I make this salad for summer parties and easy weekday lunches, I also make it for my kids' lunchboxes!

Juicy tomatoes, little balls of fresh mozzarella, and tons of basil come together with peppery arugula to dress up these tortellini, making it a go-to recipe of mine all year long. A double or triple batch is great for a cookout.

It takes only about 30 minutes to throw this together as a dinner side for grilled chicken. And a batch of it will give me close to a week's worth of lunchbox filler, which is a giant win.

Other varieties of tortellini work, too, so don't be afraid to make it your own!

Cook the tortellini according to the package directions. It only takes a few minutes, so be sure to watch it so it doesn't overcook. Drain and let it cool slightly before using.

Place the arugula in a large bowl. Toss with a pinch of salt and pepper. Add the tortellini, tomatoes, and mozzarella. Drizzle in a few spoonfuls of dressing and toss. Add the fresh basil. Taste and season more if needed. Add more dressing as desired. This stays great in the fridge for a few days.

10-Minute Meal Prep

The dressing can be made ahead of time and stored in the fridge. The tomatoes can also be chopped and stored in the fridge.

caprese cottage cheese toast

1 tablespoon extra-virgin olive oil

2 cups cherry tomatoes

2 garlic cloves, minced

1 teaspoon sugar

Kosher salt and black pepper

2 slices sourdough bread, toasted

1 cup cottage cheese

¼ cup chopped fresh basil

2 tablespoons balsamic glaze

1 tablespoon hot honey

Remember when I said I love to eat cottage cheese in a savory manner?
This is exactly how.
Burst tomatoes, fresh basil, balsamic drizzle, some flaky salt.
Done. Sold. Sign me up.
Dare I say, this almost tastes like . . . pizza?
A thick slab of sourdough bread is required for this recipe and then you can pile on your favorites. Lunch just got so much more delicious.

Heat the olive oil in a skillet over medium heat. Add the tomatoes, garlic, sugar, and a big pinch of salt and pepper. Cook, shaking the pan and stirring often, until the tomatoes burst and become almost saucy, 10 to 12 minutes. Turn off the heat.

Spread each slice of toasted sourdough with ½ cup cottage cheese. Sprinkle on some salt and pepper. Top the cottage cheese with the tomatoes. Add on the fresh basil. Drizzle each with the balsamic and hot honey. Serve!

10-Minute Meal Prep

The tomatoes can be made ahead of time and stored in a sealed container in the fridge.

hummus crunch bowls

2 cups cooked couscous

¾ cup hummus

1 cup cherry tomatoes, chopped

½ cup chopped cucumbers

½ cup chopped roasted red peppers

½ cup pitted kalamata olives

¼ cup diced red onions

2 tablespoons chopped fresh parsley

1 batch Smashed Feta Vinaigrette (page 30)

½ cup pita chips, crushed

Why does a salad seem so much more appealing when it's labeled as a "bowl"?!

And what makes a salad different from a bowl? Here, I'll tell you about mine.

For me, the base of a bowl is a grain, and while it may have some greens piled on it, they aren't the main ingredients of the salad. This hummus crunch bowl is everything I want to eat for lunch, with super-crunchy pita chips showered over it and a sprinkle of crumbly feta cheese.

Add meat, or don't. Add your favorite vegetables, or don't. A bowl is something you throw together with ingredients you love, and this is my Mediterranean version. Plus, it's a great clean-out-the-fridge meal.

It's savory, tart, and briny—my favorite mix. Paired with the creamy hummus, you can't take a wrong turn on the way to this flavor city.

Divide the couscous evenly between two bowls. Add a scoop of hummus to each. Top with the tomatoes, cucumbers, peppers, olives, onion, and parsley. Drizzle with the vinaigrette. Top with the crushed pita chips. Serve!

10-Minute Meal Prep

Make the couscous ahead of time and store it in the fridge. Make the dressing 1 to 2 days ahead of time and store it in the fridge. Chop all the vegetables the night before and store them separately in the fridge.

cherry jalapeño chicken salad

¼ cup mayonnaise

¼ cup plain Greek yogurt

1 tablespoon Dijon mustard

1 lemon, juiced

Kosher salt and black pepper

2 cups shredded cooked chicken

1 cup dried tart cherries

½ cup sliced almonds

2 jalapeño peppers, seeds removed, diced

2 scallions, sliced

1 celery rib, diced

2 tablespoons finely chopped parsley

Welcome to the best chicken salad I've ever had!

Sure, I can be dramatic. In fact, most might say I'm dramatic all the time. Especially when it comes to food. It's just that I have so many favorites. Picking a favorite ingredient, recipe, or dish is like asking me to choose a favorite child. I just can't do it!

But I *can* say with certainty that this is the best chicken salad I've ever made. It's sweet and savory. It has a very slight touch of heat. It has some chew from the tart cherries and some crunch from the almonds.

This is so wonderful served with flatbread or crackers, on a sandwich or toast, in a tortilla—there are so many ways. I want to shout it from the rooftops, and I want everyone to taste it.

You won't want to go back to traditional chicken salad after this one.

In a bowl, whisk together the mayo, yogurt, mustard, lemon juice, and a pinch of salt and pepper.

Stir in the shredded chicken, cherries, almonds, jalapeños, scallions, celery, and parsley. Taste and season more if needed. This can be stored in the fridge for up to 3 days. It tastes better as it sits.

10-Minute Meal Prep

The entire salad can be made ahead of time and stored in the fridge!

endive egg salad cups with potato chips

6 hard-boiled eggs, peeled and chopped

2½ tablespoons plain Greek yogurt

1½ tablespoons mayonnaise

1½ tablespoons dill pickle juice

2 teaspoons sweet relish

1 teaspoon Dijon mustard

3 tablespoons freshly snipped chives, plus extra for serving

Kosher salt and black pepper

⅛ teaspoon smoked paprika

8 to 12 endive leaves, washed

½ cup barbecue-flavored kettle-cooked potato chips, crushed, for serving

My egg salad is practically famous. It's one I've been making for decades now, and with a drizzle of pickle juice (yes, don't be scared), perfectly cooked eggs, and the right ratio of herbs, it's a recipe that gets rave reviews every time.

While the egg salad is fabulous, this recipe isn't necessarily about that. It's all in how we're serving it. And that includes potato chips. This preparation brings so much life to a classic egg salad, along with tons of texture and flavor.

Endive cups are required, because they are the perfect vehicle for serving the salad and holding everything in. They are also so crispy and crunchy. It's like you're making an egg salad boat.

But the topping is where things take off. And it's nothing special or fancy. Grab a bag of kettle cooked potato chips. The super crunchy kind. And crush them, then sprinkle them right on top of that egg salad boat. Alllllllll over the top.

This savory, salty shower brings even more texture to an already crisp salad boat, while turning up the flavor factor to 100%!

To boil the perfect egg, place the eggs in a large pot and fill it with cold water. Bring it to a boil and let bubble for 1 minute, then turn off the heat and cover the pot. Let the pot sit for 15 minutes. After 15 minutes, place the pot in the sink and fill it with cold water to cool down the eggs immediately.

You want the eggs to sit in cold water for about 30 minutes, so you will need to dump the water and refill with cold water a few times. You can add some ice cubes, too.

To make the salad, whisk together the yogurt, mayo, pickle juice, relish, and mustard. Gently stir in the chopped hard-boiled eggs. Fold in the chives, a big pinch of salt and pepper, and the paprika. Taste and season more if needed.

Place the endive leaves on a plate. Fill them with a few tablespoons of the egg salad (this will differ depending on the size of the endive!). Sprinkle with chives and the crushed potato chips. Serve!

10-Minute Meal Prep

The egg salad can be made up to 3 days ahead of time and stored in the fridge in a sealed container.

Serves 6 to 8 | **Time: 25 minutes**

crab salad rolls

6 to 8 top-sliced brioche buns

⅓ cup mayonnaise

3 tablespoons plain Greek yogurt or sour cream

2 tablespoons chopped fresh dill, plus more for serving

2 tablespoons chopped chives, plus more for serving

1 tablespoon Dijon mustard

1 tablespoon dill pickle relish

½ lemon, juiced

½ teaspoon Old Bay Seasoning, plus more for serving (optional)

16 ounces jumbo lump crabmeat

Kosher salt and black pepper, if needed

6 to 8 butter lettuce leaves, for serving

6 to 8 lemon wedges, for serving

Potato chips, for serving

Pickle spears, for serving

I had to include a lunch recipe that you can make for all your friends.

These crab salad rolls are what I'd consider a "fancy" lunch. This is not necessarily a recipe I'd prepare for just myself for lunch, unless of course I'm using leftovers.

But this is a dish that is wonderful to make for friends and family, when you're having people over for lunch (one of my goals every year), or even as a vacation lunch to pack for the beach.

My crab salad uses lump crabmeat—the good stuff. Lots of fresh herbs, too. It's best served in a warm and buttery brioche bun and reminds me of a lobster roll in the best way possible. But with crab!

A tray of these is beautiful on a summer holiday or cookout. The crab salad is wonderful when made ahead of time and gets even better as it sits in the fridge.

Preheat the oven to 350°F. Place the buns on a baking sheet and toast for 8 to 10 minutes, until warmed through. This is an optional step that can be skipped, but it makes the rolls extra delicious.

While the rolls are toasting, whisk together the mayonnaise, yogurt, dill, chives, mustard, relish, lemon juice, and Old Bay. Fold in the lump crabmeat until combined. Taste and season with a pinch of salt and pepper, if needed.

Open the brioche buns and layer a piece of butter lettuce on each bottom half. Divide the crab salad among the buns. Sprinkle with extra dill, chives, and Old Bay if you wish and serve with a lemon wedge for spritzing. Serve with potato chips and pickles!

10-Minute Meal Prep

The salad can be made 1 day ahead of time and stored in the fridge.

fire roasted lentil lunch soup

1 tablespoon extra-virgin olive oil

1 medium sweet onion, diced

4 garlic cloves, minced

2 large carrots, diced

1 celery rib, diced

Kosher salt and black pepper

1 teaspoon smoked paprika

1 tablespoon tomato paste

14 ounces crushed fire roasted tomatoes

28 ounces cooked canned lentils, drained and rinsed

3 to 4 cups chicken stock (see page 113)

1 Parmesan rind (2 inches in size)

Shaved Parmesan cheese, for serving

Seasoned Sourdough Croutons, for serving (page 41)

Almost every soup I make is an excellent candidate for leftovers. Sometimes, I make soup for dinner just so I can have the leftovers for lunch the next day or two.

In this case, I make this lentil soup especially for lunch, because it's so warming, delicious, and satisfying. Plus, it uses already cooked lentils, which is a giant time saver and a great way to get in good protein and fiber.

I love a lentil soup for lunch because it's so creamy, easy to heat up, doesn't include any broth-sucking pasta, and is a great soup for dipping. Give me all the baguettes, garlic toast, and rolls to dip in soup, and I am a happy camper.

I load up this soup with vegetables, heat a portion for lunch, and feel great. It's one recipe that never fails me and I have it on repeat many months out of the year.

Heat the oil in a large stockpot over medium heat. Add the onion, garlic, carrots, and celery with a big pinch of salt and pepper. Cook until the vegetables soften, 6 to 8 minutes. Stir in the paprika and tomato paste. Stir to coat the vegetables. Cook for another 2 to 3 minutes so the tomato paste can toast in the skillet.

Pour in the tomatoes, lentils, stock, and Parmesan rind. Bring the mixture to a boil. Reduce it to a simmer and cover. Simmer for 15 to 20 minutes. Taste and season additionally if needed. Top with shaved Parmesan and croutons.

10-Minute Meal Prep

The vegetables can be chopped ahead of time and stored in the fridge.

salad wraps 4 ways

rainbow kale with hummus dressing

2 burrito-size tortillas or wraps

2 cups shredded kale

½ cup sliced sweet peppers

½ cup chopped tomatoes

¼ cup sliced scallions

¼ cup chopped carrots

¼ cup corn

¼ cup Hummus Dressing (page 38)

crispy chicken cobb with green goddess ranch

2 burrito-size tortillas or wraps

2 cups chopped romaine lettuce

1 cup chopped crispy chicken (page 150)

1 hard-boiled egg, chopped

½ cup chopped tomatoes

¼ cup crumbled bacon

¼ cup crumbled blue cheese

¼ cup Green Goddess Ranch (page 26)

In college, I ate salad wraps almost every day. This sounds like a great, healthy idea. One of our dining halls specialized in salad wraps, and when I say they were bigger than the size of my head? I might even be underestimating.

The salad wraps I had in college were almost always filled with iceberg lettuce, chicken, maybe a Caesar or Italian dressing. Some tomatoes, onions, cucumbers—nothing crazy or mind-blowing. I liked eating them, though, because they were filling and loaded with greens. Made me feel better about myself in those college days.

Since then, I've perfected the salad wrap at home. I use large tortillas or lavash wraps and pile everything on there. Meat is optional and you can always change up a few ingredients!

My kids love these, too, which makes me happy because, again, it's an easy way to get some vegetables.

Below you'll find four of my most popular salad wraps. And let's just say that they are ALL so good. I can't even pick a favorite.

To make a salad wrap with any of these salads, combine all the ingredients (except the wraps!) in a bowl, tossing well. Drizzle with the dressing and toss again, so everything is coated. Heat the tortilla in the microwave for a few seconds or in a 350°F oven for 1 minute.

Divide the salad mixture between two wraps, placing it right in the center of the wrap. Fold up the top and the bottom of the tortilla, then roll the sides in tightly to wrap it up.

10-Minute Meal Prep

For all the salad wraps, the ingredients can be chopped and stored separately in the fridge 1 to 2 days ahead of time until ready to use.

italian chopped

2 burrito-size tortillas or wraps

2 cups chopped butter lettuce

½ cup chopped salami

½ cup cooked chickpeas

½ cup chopped cucumber

½ cup chopped roasted red peppers

¼ cup chopped banana peppers

¼ cup chopped red onions

¼ cup shaved Parmesan cheese

3 tablespoons chopped fresh parsley

¼ cup My Go-To Zesty Italian Dressing (page 44)

my favorite caesar

2 burrito-size tortillas or wraps

4 cups chopped romaine lettuce

½ cup shaved Parmesan cheese

½ cup Seasoned Sourdough Croutons (page 41)

¼ cup Lemon Caesar Dressing (page 34)

CHAPTER 4

dinners
& sides

There's a certain kind of dinner magic that I've been chasing most of my adult life. That's the only way I can describe it. Growing up, my parents, especially my mom, made dinnertime feel magical almost every night.

Of course, I didn't realize it then. It wasn't until I reached a certain age, and definitely once I had kids, that I realized just how incredible it was that my parents managed to get us around the dinner table every single night.

And the thing was that my mom made it look *effortless*.

Now that I'm a mom myself, I know that there is no way it actually was effortless for her. In no world did feeding a family of five, full of activities, school, work and play, along with a few picky eaters, manage to be effortless.

But that has become my goal. To make meals for my family that we all enjoy. Ones that don't take very long, ones with mostly simple ingredients, ones I can throw together on a busy school night, that we can all enjoy around the table.

A repertoire of meals like this can make dinnertime almost feel effortless today, and that's the goal.

In this chapter, you'll find a whole host of our favorites. Dinnertime is my bread and butter. It's where my favorite meals lie; it's what I'm passionate about. I always want to have nourishing, seasonal, and fresh ingredients on hand so I can bring meals together quickly. Meals that make us feel good.

Some of these recipes are also a one-stop shop: They include a main entrée and a side dish. My mom was the queen of the side dish—she had *at least* two sides every night at dinner. So, while I may provide a recipe for chicken and rice, or meatballs and mashed potatoes, or chili and cornbread, I suggest adding more if you wish.

To make dinner easy, I keep a list of vegetable sides we love in the notes section of my phone. These are simple vegetable sides, like roasted broccoli or asparagus with Parmesan—and I rotate through them when I need to add something to our meal. It's an easy hack for dinner and one that pleases everyone!

Can't wait for you to cook some of my faves from this chapter. It's where all the good stuff lies. ●

simple whole roasted chicken

1 medium sweet onion, thinly sliced

1 lemon, sliced

4- to 5-pound whole chicken

2 to 3 tablespoons extra-virgin olive oil

Kosher salt and black pepper

I've been making this simple version of a roasted chicken for more than fifteen years. Pretty much since I got married, when I discovered the wonderful world of whole roasted chicken and realized it *really isn't that difficult!*

The flavors are simple. I do not stuff butter and herbs up under the skin for this chicken, even though *that* is absolutely delicious. I don't do anything fancy with garlic. I simply roast this at 425°F and it's PERFECT.

The skin is ridiculously crispy. It's perfect to pull for sandwiches and soups the next day.

Making a whole chicken is something I do for meal prep constantly. It is easy and barely takes any hands-on time. I promise that once you do it a few times, it becomes like second nature. Plus, your house will smell incredible.

We use the chicken for all sorts of recipes, much like you would a rotisserie chicken you grab at the grocery store. I sometimes roast two or three chickens at once, pull off the meat, and toss it in the freezer when I'm doing some meal prep. I'll use the carcass to make chicken stock, which is another excellent idea (see page 113). These are time-saving tricks that save my dinner-life!

Preheat the oven to 425°F.

Place the onion and lemon slices in a 9 × 13-inch baking dish or a 10-inch cast-iron pan. Place the whole chicken on top, breast-side down. I like to put it breast-side down because this way, the juices run into the breast, making the meat juicier.

Rub the chicken all over with the olive oil. Season it all over with a big pinch of salt and pepper.

Stick the dish in the oven. Roast, uncovered, for 60 to 70 minutes. Remove the chicken and take the internal temperature—you want it to read 165°F. If the chicken is still not finished, roast in 10-minute increments until it is done.

Let the chicken rest for 20 to 30 minutes before slicing or pulling the meat off the bones.

10-Minute Meal Prep

The onion and lemon can be sliced ahead of time and stored in the fridge.

To make a slightly fancier version of this chicken, stir together 6 tablespoons of softened butter with ¼ cup of chopped fresh herbs (rosemary, thyme, parsley, chives, basil) and 2 minced garlic cloves. Stuff this butter-herb mixture up under the chicken skin on the breast and legs before roasting. Follow the same instructions to roast.

bonus: make the best chicken stock!

Don't let that chicken carcass go to waste. Heat 1 tablespoon of olive oil in a large stockpot over medium heat. Add 2 onions (cut in half), 2 carrots (cut into thirds), and 2 celery ribs (cut into thirds) to the oil with a big pinch of kosher salt and pepper. Cook, stirring occasionally, until the vegetables soften and get some golden color on them.

Add the chicken carcass, a few sprigs each of fresh rosemary and thyme, and a bunch of fresh parsley. Add 8 to 10 cups of cold water. Bring the mixture to a boil. Skim off any foam that comes to the surface. Reduce to a simmer, cover, and cook for 2 to 3 hours.

Let cool completely. Strain the mixture a few times through a fine-mesh strainer, removing all bits. Store in the fridge for 4 to 5 days or in the freezer for 3 to 4 months.

cilantro lime grilled chicken bowl

1 pound boneless, skinless chicken breasts

1 batch Cilantro Lime Dressing (page 29)

2 cups cooked jasmine rice

1 cup chopped tomatoes

⅔ cup sweet corn (fresh or frozen corn works)

1 avocado, chopped

Quick Pickled Onions (page 40)

Kosher salt and black pepper (optional)

These grilled chicken bowls are versatile and can include anything you want. I love serving the chicken over rice, but feel free to use a different grain. In the summer, corn and tomatoes are perfect here. In the cooler months, sweet potatoes, radishes, and leeks are delish.

The cilantro lime dressing here might be my favorite dressing of all time. It tastes wonderful, and it's equally delicious as a marinade or as a salad or bowl dressing. And it's a vibrantly gorgeous shade of green that makes me so happy.

This dish takes a bit longer due to the marinating time for the chicken, but it's totally worth it.

I use the dressing as both a marinade AND a drizzle here, so sometimes I'll double the amount I make. Once you taste it, you'll probably feel the same!

Place the chicken in a baking dish or resealable bag. Pour half of the cilantro lime dressing over the chicken, making sure each piece is coated. Cover and let the chicken marinate in the fridge for at least 30 minutes or up to 2 hours. You can even marinate overnight. Place the remaining dressing in the fridge.

Remove the chicken from the fridge about 20 minutes before you're ready to make it. Preheat the grill to the highest heat for at least 10 minutes. I like mine between 500 to 550°F!

Remove the chicken from the marinade and let any excess drip off. Place the chicken on the grates and grill for 5 to 6 minutes per side, or until the internal temperature reaches 165°F. If you're using corn on the cob, you can also throw the ears of corn directly on the grill grates!

Let the chicken rest for 5 to 10 minutes before slicing or chopping it.

To assemble the meal, place the rice in a large bowl. Drizzle in some of the cilantro lime dressing and toss well. Divide the rice among two or four bowls. Top each bowl with some of the grilled chicken, corn, tomatoes, avocado, and pickled onions. Drizzle with any extra dressing and sprinkle on salt and pepper if desired. Serve!

10-Minute Meal Prep

The cilantro lime dressing can be made ahead of time. The rice can be cooked ahead of time, or this is a great recipe to use leftover rice. The chicken can also marinate overnight!

crispy potato tacos

2 pounds baby Yukon Gold potatoes

1 teaspoon smoked paprika

½ teaspoon ground cumin

½ teaspoon garlic powder

Kosher salt and black pepper

2 tablespoons avocado oil or another high-heat oil

8 small flour tortillas

4 ounces freshly grated white Cheddar cheese

½ cup sour cream

1 lime, juiced

1 teaspoon chipotle chili powder

Quick Pickled Onions (page 40), for serving

Chili Pepita Crunch (page 47), for serving

¼ cup crumbled cotija cheese, for serving

10-Minute Meal Prep

The chipotle sour cream can be made ahead of time. The spices can be stirred together, the cheese can be grated, and, of course, both the pickled onions and pepita crunch work best when made ahead and stored in the fridge.

We've vacationed in northern Michigan my entire life, in a small town that my dad's grandparents called home. It's my favorite place on earth, and years ago we discovered a taco truck there that serves crispy potato tacos.

I dream of these tacos. Having them once a year is not nearly enough, so I started making my own version at home. A cheesy tortilla is key. Crispy, pan-roasted potatoes that you can make in a short time. And a pepita crunch on top that is spicy, crunchy, and savory really takes the whole thing over the top.

I've tried many meat-free tacos in my day, but these take the cake. They are so crunchy and cheesy and a huge crowd-pleaser. I can never get enough!

Preheat the oven to 350°F.

Chop the potatoes into halves or quarters, depending on their size. You want the potato pieces to be as equal in size as possible.

Toss the potatoes with the paprika, cumin, garlic powder, and a big pinch of salt and pepper. Toss until all the pieces are coated in the spices.

Heat the oil in a large skillet (that has a tight-fitting lid) over medium heat. Add the potatoes to the skillet in a single layer. Cover and let cook for 15 to 20 minutes without disturbing the potatoes so they get very golden and crisp.

In a small bowl, whisk together the sour cream, lime juice, and chipotle chili powder.

Remove the lid from the potatoes and gently flip them. Once all the potatoes are flipped, cover again and cook for another 8 to 10 minutes, until they are all fork-tender and golden.

While the potatoes cook, place the tortillas on a baking sheet. Divide the Cheddar cheese evenly among the tortillas, sprinkling it in the middle. Place the tortillas in the oven for 5 to 8 minutes, until the cheese melts and the tortillas are warm.

To assemble the tacos, divide the potatoes equally among the tortillas, right on top of the melted cheese. Add a drizzle of the sour cream mixture, some pickled onions, and a spoonful of pepita crunch. Sprinkle with the cotija cheese. Serve!

chicken zucchini meatballs with lemon rice

meatballs

1 pound ground chicken
(I like 93% lean)

1 cup grated zucchini

4 garlic cloves, minced

1 large egg, lightly beaten

⅓ cup seasoned bread crumbs

¼ cup finely grated Parmesan
cheese

¼ cup chopped fresh parsley,
plus more for serving

2 tablespoons dried chives

Kosher salt and black pepper

2 tablespoons extra-virgin olive oil

lemon rice

3 cups chicken stock (see page 113)

1 tablespoon salted butter

Kosher salt and black pepper

1 cup dry jasmine rice

2 tablespoons fresh lemon zest

2 tablespoons fresh lemon juice

10-Minute Meal Prep

The meatballs can be formed ahead of time and stored in the fridge. They can also be flash frozen, meaning you can roll them, place on a baking sheet, freeze for 1 hour, and then transfer them to a bag or container and keep in the freezer for up to 3 months.

The rice can also be made ahead of time!

Meatballs are dinner gold in our house. They are equally loved by everyone. We're talking about all versions of meatballs. Ground beef, chicken, turkey—a variety of flavors and textures—we don't discriminate.

These chicken meatballs are loaded with flavor and lots of shredded zucchini. Not only is this a great way to get in some vegetables, the zucchini also provides a moisture level to the meatballs that you really can't find elsewhere. These savory little bites are fabulous on their own, dipped in a sauce, or, as I like to make for dinner, with creamy lemon rice.

This lemon rice may become a staple side dish, too. I make it with Crispy Chicken with Broccoli Slaw (see page 152) and it's as tasty as it is simple.

This plate gets a big thumbs up from everyone here!

to make the meatballs Preheat the oven to 350°F.

In a large bowl, combine the chicken, zucchini, garlic, egg, bread crumbs, Parmesan, parsley, chives, and a big pinch of salt and pepper.

Use your hands to mix the meatballs until combined, being careful not to overmix. Form the mixture into meatballs that are roughly 1 inch in size.

Heat the olive oil in an oven-safe skillet over medium heat. Once hot, add the meatballs in a single layer and brown on all sides, about 2 minutes each side.

Transfer the skillet to the oven. Cook for 8 to 12 minutes, or until the internal temperature reaches 165°F.

Remove the skillet and serve the meatballs over the lemon rice. Sprinkle with fresh parsley.

to make the lemon rice Heat the chicken stock in a large saucepan over medium heat. Add the butter and a big pinch of salt and pepper. Once boiling, add the rice.

Bring the mixture to a boil again, then reduce it to a simmer. Cover and cook for 12 to 15 minutes, or until the liquid is absorbed.

Remove the lid and stir in the lemon zest and juice. Serve with the meatballs.

triple berry avocado arugula salad

10 ounces baby arugula

Kosher salt and black pepper

1 cup strawberries, quartered

1 cup blackberries

⅔ cup blueberries

⅓ cup crumbled blue cheese

⅓ cup sliced almonds

3 tablespoons chopped fresh mint

1 avocado, thinly sliced

1 batch Champagne Vinaigrette (page 33)

I am very much "team fruit" in salad. I love making seasonal salads with fruit, whether it's berries, apples, pears, persimmon, or even watermelon. I love the pop of flavor and sweetness the fruit brings. And it complements greens, nuts, and cheese very well.

This triple berry salad is my go-to in the summer. Whether I'm looking for a side salad for dinner, a great base to use under grilled chicken or steak, or a big salad that I want to take to a Fourth of July barbecue, this one always fits the bill.

It's so beautiful and vibrant. It's tart, sweet, creamy, cheesy, and peppery. It's also very popular with the kids because of all the berries.

And my favorite part is that it works with a variety of dressings, too! You can't go wrong with this one.

Add the arugula to a large bowl. Season all over with a big pinch of salt and pepper and toss.

Add the berries, blue cheese, almonds, mint, and avocado. Add another pinch of salt and pepper on the avocado.

Drizzle on the champagne vinaigrette and serve.

10-Minute Meal Prep

The strawberries can be quartered ahead of time. The dressing can be made ahead of time, too.

weeknight baked penne with spinach

1 (32-ounce) jar marinara sauce

1 tablespoon extra-virgin olive oil

4 garlic cloves, minced

1 pound ground turkey

Kosher salt and black pepper

8 ounces fresh spinach

1 pound cooked penne

8 ounces shredded mozzarella or Italian cheese blend

8 ounces fresh mozzarella

Freshly grated Parmesan cheese, for serving

Chopped fresh herbs, like parsley, for serving

This is one of my cop-out meals, as Eddie likes to say. It's one of my super-easy, throw together, make-often, classic meals that everyone loves. Pasta, sauce, cheese, and greens. There is nothing else we need!

This easy recipe isn't anything groundbreaking, but it's one that we get excited about every time it's on the table for dinner. All it takes is a pound of cooked pasta, browned ground turkey, your favorite marinara sauce, a lot of fresh or frozen spinach, and some mozzarella cheese.

When baked, this turns into a cheesy, bubbly dish of comfort food that no one can deny. It's heavenly with a salad. Leftovers are irresistible. It's everyone's favorite for a reason!

Preheat the oven to 400°F. Reserve 1 cup of marinara sauce from the jar.

Heat the oil in a large nonstick skillet over medium-low heat. Stir in the garlic and cook for 30 seconds. Add the turkey with a big pinch of salt and pepper. Cook until the turkey is browned, 6 to 8 minutes, breaking it apart into small crumbles. Once the turkey is browned all over, add the rest of the marinara from the jar.

Once the marinara is warm and bubbling, stir in the spinach. Cook for a few minutes, until the spinach wilts, and then turn off the heat.

Time to layer! Add ½ cup of the reserved marinara in the bottom of a 9 × 13-inch baking dish and spread it around. Add a layer of penne. Next, add a layer of the ground turkey/spinach mixture. You want to use a third of the mixture. Sprinkle on some of the grated cheese. Repeat this two more times, so you have three layers total.

Once you finish the final layer, add the remaining ½ cup of marinara on top. Top with any extra grated cheese. Top with the fresh mozzarella, pulling it apart to spread it out over the entire dish.

Bake for 25 to 30 minutes, until golden and bubbly and cheesy and melty! Top with Parmesan and fresh herbs. Serve! This stays great in the fridge for 3 to 4 days.

10-Minute Meal Prep

The cheese can be grated ahead of time. The ground turkey marinara can also be made ahead of time and stored in the fridge for 2 to 3 days. The penne can be cooked ahead of time, tossed with a drop of olive oil, and stored in the fridge in a resealable bag.

shaved asiago house salad

10 ounces spring greens

Kosher salt and black pepper

½ cup shaved asiago cheese

2 medium carrots, peeled and grated

1½ cups halved cherry tomatoes

1 cup sliced mini sweet peppers

¼ cup diced red onions

¼ cup roasted, salted sunflower seeds

½ cup Seasoned Sourdough Croutons (page 41)

1 batch My Go-To Zesty Italian Dressing (page 44)

I live for a good house salad.

For some reason, a few years ago I became obsessed with the idea of having a signature house salad. An incredible, flavorful, green salad filled with everyday ingredients that tastes wonderful with almost every recipe.

And that's what we have here.

This salad is full of ingredients that you probably have in your fridge, but there are two stand-outs that make quite the difference: shaved asiago cheese and roasted sunflower seeds. The cheese provides a buttery nuttiness that is so good in a salad—especially when it's shaved with a vegetable peeler. The paper-thin slices mesh so nicely with the lettuce that you get a great bite every time. The roasted sunflower seeds provide even more nutty flavor with the best bit of crunch. Because they aren't as large as a walnut or a pecan, kids usually like this salad.

Finally, I serve this with my zesty Italian dressing. But it's such a classic that you can really use any dressing on top. And serve it next to any recipe, too!

Place the spring greens in a large bowl and toss with a big pinch of salt and pepper. The key to a delicious salad is seasoning the lettuce! I also like to take a handful of the shaved asiago cheese and toss it in with the greens.

Add the carrots, tomatoes, peppers, onions, and sunflower seeds. Top with the remaining asiago cheese and the croutons.

Drizzle with the dressing and serve!

10-Minute Meal Prep

The vegetables can be chopped the night before and stored separately in the fridge. The dressing can be made a few days before and stored in the fridge.

lemon spaghetti
with roasted chickpeas

chickpeas

1 (15-ounce) can chickpeas, drained and rinsed

1 tablespoon extra-virgin olive oil

1 teaspoon smoked paprika

1 teaspoon garlic powder

½ teaspoon dried oregano

½ teaspoon kosher salt

½ teaspoon freshly cracked black pepper

pasta

1 pound spaghetti

⅓ cup extra-virgin olive oil

2 tablespoons fresh lemon zest

3 tablespoons fresh lemon juice

Kosher salt and black pepper

⅓ cup finely grated Parmesan cheese, plus more for serving

Chopped fresh herbs, like parsley and basil, for serving

10-Minute Meal Prep

The chickpeas can be roasted 1 day ahead of time and stored in a container until ready to use. They may lose a bit of their crispness when roasted ahead.

If you're noticing a theme here, you're probably right: I really love lemon.

Lemon brightens so many dishes in a refreshing way. And it's an easy and economical way to add acid to foods, which is a major factor to upping the flavor profile. Plus, it's loved by many people. It's a beautiful ingredient because using it doesn't always make things taste overwhelmingly like lemon.

But in this case, I want my spaghetti to taste like lemon. And it does in the most wonderful way. This creamy lemon bucatini is mouthwateringly delicious. You can serve it with grilled chicken or even steak filet, but I love to make a sheet pan of roasted chickpeas and throw them on top.

Oh, the crunch!

The crunch and the flavor are out of this world. The texture of the chickpeas complements the creamy pasta so much. And you get a bite of everything with each fork twirl.

make the chickpeas   Preheat the oven to 425°F.

Place the chickpeas on a towel and lightly towel-dry them so they aren't wet from rinsing. You can remove any loose skins at this time, too.

Place the chickpeas on a baking sheet and drizzle with the olive oil. Toss to coat, then sprinkle with the paprika, garlic powder, oregano, salt, and pepper. Shake the pan a few times to distribute the seasoning. Roast the chickpeas for 15 minutes, then toss and roast for 10 to 15 minutes more, until they are golden in color.

make the pasta   While the chickpeas are roasting, bring a large pot of salted water to a boil. Cook the pasta according to the directions, reserving ½ cup of the starchy pasta water when finished.

In a large bowl (one large enough to add the pasta), whisk together the olive oil, lemon zest and juice, a big pinch of salt and pepper, and the Parmesan. Add the hot pasta directly to the bowl and toss, making sure that every strand is coated.

Drizzle in the pasta water and continue to toss. Taste and add more salt and pepper if needed.

Serve the pasta with the roasted chickpeas on top, sprinkled with additional Parmesan and fresh herbs.

hot honey apricot chicken with pan-toasted broccoli

1½ pounds boneless, skinless chicken thighs

Kosher salt and black pepper

1 teaspoon garlic powder

⅓ cup apricot preserves

3 tablespoons apple cider vinegar

1 tablespoon hot honey

pan-toasted butter broccoli

2 tablespoons unsalted butter

4 cups broccoli florets

Kosher salt and black pepper

2 garlic cloves, minced

3 tablespoons water

10-Minute Meal Prep

The apricot mixture can be combined a day ahead of time and stored in the fridge.

I've unlocked the secret to sheet pan meals and I'm going to share it with you.

Gone are the days of throwing everything on a sheet pan at once. It just doesn't cook your food evenly. The meal is always lackluster. Not to mention, it usually . . . tastes all the same.

Don't get me wrong, I'm all for a meal with complementary flavors. But in order to make a sheet pan meal work, especially one with meat and vegetables, they must be added to the sheet pan at different times.

In this case, I roast my chicken with hot honey and apricot preserves. When it has about 15 minutes left, I toss the vegetables on the pan. When the time is up, everything on the pan is cooked how it should be. The chicken is tender and the vegetables still have that crisp, al dente bite without being mushy.

The sweet and savory flavor here is everything, and this pairs wonderfully with rice or another grain you love.

Preheat the broiler in your oven to the highest setting. Make sure there is an oven rack directly beneath it.

Place the chicken on a baking sheet in a single layer. Liberally season the chicken all over with salt and pepper. Sprinkle with the garlic powder.

Place directly under the broiler for 7 minutes. Remove the pan and flip the chicken, broiling for 7 minutes more. While the chicken is broiling, whisk together the apricot preserves, vinegar, and honey in a small bowl.

After 7 minutes, remove the pan and use a pastry brush to brush the apricot mixture on the chicken. Broil for 1 minute. Remove the pan, flip the chicken, brush with the apricot mixture, and broil for another minute. Repeat one or two more times on both sides until the chicken is charred and caramelly and cooked through, reaching an internal temperature of 165°F. If there is any apricot mixture left, you can brush it on right before serving.

make the pan-toasted broccoli Heat the butter in a skillet over medium heat. Add the broccoli florets and a big pinch of salt and pepper. Cook, stirring often, for 4 to 5 minutes as the broccoli toasts in the skillet. Stir in the garlic and water. Cover and cook for about 5 minutes more, until the broccoli is tender. Serve with the chicken.

quick & easy
ricotta pesto pasta

1 pound short-cut pasta, such as penne, farfalle, etc.

15 ounces ricotta cheese

½ cup Our All-time Favorite Basil Pesto (page 35)

⅓ cup finely grated Parmesan cheese, plus more for serving

1 teaspoon fresh lemon juice

Kosher salt and black pepper

Chopped fresh basil, for serving

You will not even *believe* how quickly this meal comes together. Just wait!

Boil your pasta. Whisk together your ricotta, pesto, and cheese. Stir the pasta into the ricotta mixture. Serve it. And done!

Bring a pot of salted water to a boil and cook the pasta according to the package directions. Reserve ⅓ cup of the starchy pasta water.

While the pasta is cooking, whisk together the ricotta, pesto, Parmesan, lemon juice, and a big pinch of salt and pepper in a large bowl.

Whisk the pasta water into the ricotta mixture. Drain the pasta and immediately add the hot pasta to the bowl with the ricotta and pesto. Fold the pasta into the ricotta and stir until combined. Taste and season with more salt and pepper if needed.

Top with additional Parmesan and fresh basil. Serve!

10-Minute Meal Prep

The pesto can be made ahead of time. The pasta can be cooked a day ahead of time, but remember to reserve the water and store it in the fridge. Reheat the pasta (and the water!) until hot before making the dish.

roasted chicken & potatoes with piccata vinaigrette

1 medium sweet onion, sliced

4 garlic cloves, minced

1 pound boneless, skinless chicken thighs

2 pounds Yukon Gold baby potatoes, halved

1 lemon, sliced

Kosher salt and black pepper

2 tablespoons extra-virgin olive oil

¼ cup chicken stock (see page 113)

1 batch Piccata Vinaigrette (page 27), plus extra for serving

One of my local restaurants serves a dish like this and my entire family loves it.

Instead of the classic chicken piccata, you're going to roast chicken and potatoes together with some lemon and then drizzle a piccata vinaigrette over the entire thing.

This is a dinner dream.

If you love a fall-apart-tender chicken, crisp potatoes, and a tart, briny vinaigrette, you will love this. This meal still has that melt-in-your-mouth feel that you get from classic chicken piccata. But it's a whole meal made in one dish, plus the vinaigrette, and is an excellent, satisfying comfort food.

The vinaigrette is also incredible on things like potato salad, green salads, and any roasted vegetables. I love to keep it in the fridge in the winter months to brighten up my lunches, too!

Preheat the oven to 400°F. Spray a 9 × 13-inch baking dish with nonstick spray.

Layer the onions and garlic in the baking dish. Place the chicken thighs on top of the onions, then scatter the potatoes around the chicken. Add the lemon slices.

Season everything with a few pinches of salt and pepper. Drizzle with the olive oil. Sometimes I will give everything a good spray with olive oil so the potatoes and chicken are coated evenly. Pour the stock into the dish.

Roast for 45 to 60 minutes, until the chicken reaches 165°F and the potatoes are fork-tender.

Remove the dish from the oven and spoon the vinaigrette over everything. Serve with extra vinaigrette.

10-Minute Meal Prep

The vinaigrette can be made 1 to 2 days ahead of time. The onion can also be sliced and stored in the fridge.

smashburger salad

2 tablespoons unsalted butter

1 pound lean ground beef

Kosher salt and black pepper

4 slices sharp white Cheddar cheese

10 ounces butter lettuce leaves

1½ cups cherry tomatoes, halved

½ cup chopped pickles

Caramelized Shallot Dressing
(page 25)

I live for a good smashburger. Those ragged, paper-thin edges of the burger, with deeply golden bits from being smashed into sizzling butter—oh my gosh. It might be my favorite meal!

Which is why I turned it into a salad.

A cheeseburger salad is nothing new, but a smashburger salad is one million times better. Instead of crumbly ground beef or thick burger patties, we have thin slabs of smashburger with the classic shaggy edges, topped with melty cheese.

And the vinaigrette takes it over the top. Caramelized shallot dressing drizzled all over the greens adds such incredible flavor that you won't even be able to stand it.

This is my #1 requested salad by friends and family. Make it and find out why!

Melt the butter in a large cast-iron skillet over medium heat. Meanwhile, season the ground beef with lots of salt and pepper, then divide it into four pieces.

Once the skillet is hot and the butter is melted, press each piece of ground beef into the skillet, using the bottom of a jar or spatula to smash it into the skillet. Cook for 5 to 6 minutes, then flip and smash the other side into the skillet. Cook for another 2 to 3 minutes. You want golden, crisp edges!

Place a piece of Cheddar over each smashburger. Let it melt completely, then remove the burgers from the skillet.

Place the lettuce in a bowl and toss it with a big pinch of salt and pepper. Add the tomatoes and pickles. Tear or cut the smashburgers into pieces and scatter them over the salad.

Drizzle with the caramelized shallot vinaigrette and serve!

10-Minute Meal Prep

The dressing can be made ahead of time and stored in the fridge. Just let it come to room temperature or warm it in the microwave before serving.

sun-dried tomato baked shrimp with artichokes

1 pound raw jumbo shrimp, peeled and deveined

Kosher salt and black pepper

1 (12-ounce) jar marinated artichoke hearts, drained

1 (7-ounce) jar sun-dried tomatoes in oil, drained, with 2 tablespoons oil reserved

2 garlic cloves, minced

8 ounces feta cheese, cut into cubes

1 lemon, sliced

¼ cup chopped fresh parsley, for serving

½ teaspoon crushed red pepper flakes, for serving

1 baguette, for serving

I make this baked shrimp dish for practically one reason alone: to drag crusty sourdough bread through the pan and get all the bits of flavor.

Okay, I'm kidding. But really not. That's partially why I love this recipe. It's light and easy, a great throw-together dish. It reminds me of some of the seafood dishes my dad would prepare when I was a kid. All the flavors work so well together and the plump, buttery shrimp is fantastic.

Plus, the bread. Just don't forget the bread.

Preheat the oven to 400°F. Spray a 9 × 13-inch baking dish with nonstick spray.

Season the shrimp all over with salt and pepper. Layer the shrimp in the baking dish with the artichoke hearts and sun-dried tomatoes. There is no exact method here, just scatter them around each other!

Sprinkle on the garlic cloves and cubes of feta. Scatter the lemon slices around the dish.

Drizzle the shrimp with the reserved oil from the jar of tomatoes.

Bake for 12 to 15 minutes, or until the shrimp is opaque and cooked through.

Remove from the oven and top with a sprinkling of fresh parsley and red pepper flakes. Serve with the baguette!

10-Minute Meal Prep

The shrimp can be peeled and deveined ahead of time if needed. The artichokes and tomatoes can be drained (don't forget to reserve the oil!), the feta can be chopped, and everything can be stored in the fridge until ready to use.

blackened salmon burgers with mango slaw

1 pound boneless, skinless salmon fillet

1 shallot, minced

2 garlic cloves, minced

1 large egg

⅓ cup seasoned bread crumbs

1 teaspoon smoked paprika

½ teaspoon dried oregano

½ teaspoon garlic powder

Pinch of crushed red pepper flakes

Kosher salt and black pepper

2 tablespoons chopped fresh parsley

3 to 4 tablespoons extra-virgin olive oil

4 brioche buns, for serving

mango slaw

1 small head of cabbage, thinly sliced

1 mango, thinly sliced

½ medium red onion, thinly sliced

½ cup chopped fresh cilantro

3 tablespoons freshly squeezed lime juice

⅓ cup extra-virgin olive oil

1 tablespoon honey

Kosher salt and black pepper

10-Minute Meal Prep

The salmon burgers can be formed ahead of time and kept in the fridge or freezer. The mango slaw can be made ahead of time and stored in the fridge until ready to dress and eat.

We eat a lot of salmon in our house. It might be my favorite source of protein and I'm always looking for new and exciting ways to cook it.

On days when I'm sick of roasting or grilling it, I add it to my food processor and make salmon burgers. I first shared my Bang Bang Salmon Burger in my last cookbook, *Everyday Dinners*, and this is another favorite preparation of mine.

Blackened seasoning on salmon patties, cooked in butter until crisp on the outside and butter on the inside. Then served on a bun, piled high with refreshing, cilantro-y slaw. The texture is incredible, the flavor is right on. These hit the spot when you're craving something comforting and satisfying!

Add the salmon fillet (I cut mine into four pieces) to the food processor. Pulse until it is in small pieces but not completely ground up. Remove the salmon and put it in a large bowl. Add the shallot, garlic, egg, bread crumbs, paprika, oregano, garlic powder, red pepper flakes, a big pinch of salt and pepper, and the parsley to the bowl. Stir with a large spoon to combine, then bring the mixture together with your hands. Form the mixture into four burgers or eight sliders—or however many you want so they fit the size of your buns!

Heat a large skillet over medium heat and add 2 tablespoons of the olive oil. Add the burgers (I do it in two batches) and cook on both sides until golden brown, 4 to 5 minutes per side. You want the insides of the burgers to be opaque, so I usually turn down the heat to low and cover the skillet for another 1 to 2 minutes to ensure they are cooked through.

make the mango slaw   Place the cabbage, mango, onion, and cilantro in a large bowl. In a small bowl, whisk together the lime juice, olive oil, and honey with a pinch of salt and pepper. Season the slaw all over with salt and pepper, too. Pour the dressing over the slaw, tossing it together. Let it sit for 5 minutes and toss it again. Serve on top of the salmon burgers.

sticky bbq meatballs with herbed smashed potatoes

1 pound ground turkey

1 large egg, lightly beaten

2 garlic cloves, minced

2 scallions, thinly sliced, plus more for serving

⅓ cup seasoned bread crumbs

½ teaspoon smoked paprika

Kosher salt and black pepper

1 tablespoon extra-virgin olive oil

1 cup barbecue sauce

¼ cup honey

¼ cup water

herbed smashed potatoes

3 pounds baby Yukon Gold potatoes

Kosher salt and black pepper

6 tablespoons (¾ stick) unsalted butter

2 garlic cloves, minced

3 tablespoons chopped fresh rosemary

10-Minute Meal Prep

The meatballs can be formed ahead of time and kept in the fridge or freezer. The potatoes can be sliced 12 hours ahead of time and kept in a bowl of ice water in the fridge.

What do you get when you take round little meatballs and swirl them in a mixture of honey and barbecue sauce? You get the best dinner ever. Especially if you serve them on top of herby and buttery smashed potatoes. Comfort food is the name of the game here and I've got you covered.

Want a winner of a meal? Make this one.

In a large bowl, combine the turkey with the egg, garlic, scallions, bread crumbs, paprika, and a big pinch of salt and pepper. Mix until just combined and form the mixture into small meatballs. (Or large meatballs! Whatever you prefer!)

Heat the olive oil in a large nonstick skillet over medium heat. Add the meatballs in a single layer and brown on all sides. Once browned, transfer the meatballs to a plate.

In the same skillet, add the barbecue sauce, honey, and water. Whisk it together. Bring the mixture to a simmer. Cook for 1 minute. Add the meatballs back in and cook for a few more minutes until the sauce thickens. You want the internal temperature of the meatballs to reach 165°F before serving. Sprinkle with more scallions.

Serve with the smashed potatoes.

make the herbed smashed potatoes   Fill a large pot with the potatoes, cover them with cold water, and add a few pinches of salt. Bring to a boil. Cook for 10 to 15 minutes, or until the potatoes are fork-tender.

Melt the butter in a small saucepan over medium heat. Once melted, add the garlic and rosemary. Turn off the heat.

Once the potatoes are tender, drain the water and add the potatoes back to the pot. Begin to mash them (skin and all!) with a potato masher or fork. Stream in the melted rosemary butter. Add a big pinch of salt and pepper. Smash some more and taste. If desired, season with more salt and pepper. Serve with the meatballs.

chicken gorgonzola

2 tablespoons extra-virgin olive oil

4 boneless, skinless chicken breasts

Kosher salt and black pepper

1 medium sweet onion, diced

4 garlic cloves, minced

10 ounces cremini mushrooms, sliced

5 ounces baby spinach

1 cup heavy cream

¼ teaspoon freshly grated nutmeg

½ cup crumbled Gorgonzola cheese

Cooked rice, pasta, or vegetables, for serving

This recipe is for my mom! Every month or so, she orders this dish from a local restaurant and raves about it. It's my version of the "marry me chicken" that takes over the internet every few years, and let me just say that I could propose to myself after eating it. It's creamy. It's cheesy. The mushrooms are earthy in such a lovely way, the spinach melts into the sauce, and the chicken falls apart.

This is a decadent meal, one that is best served over rice or potatoes. You know, some sort of grain or ingredient to help soak up that delicious cream sauce. It's indulgent and wonderful, and I love making this for a cozy, wintry meal or on a special occasion.

Preheat the oven to 400°F.

Heat the olive oil in a large oven-safe skillet or Dutch oven over medium heat. Season the chicken all over with salt and pepper.

Place the chicken in the skillet and sear on both sides until deeply golden, 3 to 4 minutes per side. Transfer the chicken to a plate.

To the same skillet, stir in the onion and garlic. Cook for about 5 minutes, until softened. Stir in the mushrooms. Cook for 5 to 6 minutes more, until the mushrooms soften. Stir in the spinach. It will look like a LOT of spinach, but within a few minutes it will cook down.

Once the spinach has cooked down a bit, stir in the cream. Mix in a pinch of salt and pepper and the nutmeg.

Transfer the chicken back to the skillet, nestling it in with the spinach and mushrooms. Top the chicken with the crumbled Gorgonzola.

Place the pan in the oven and cook for about 15 minutes, until the internal temperature of the chicken reads 165°F.

Serve with rice, pasta, or vegetables.

10-Minute Meal Prep

Both the onion and mushrooms can be chopped ahead of time and stored in the fridge.

roasted cauliflower steaks with herby goat cheese

1 large head of cauliflower

3 to 4 tablespoons extra-virgin olive oil

Kosher salt and black pepper

1 teaspoon crushed red pepper flakes

3 tablespoons chopped pistachios, for serving

herby goat cheese

4 ounces goat cheese, at room temperature

1 tablespoon extra-virgin olive oil

1 tablespoon chives, plus more for serving

1 teaspoon dried rosemary

1 teaspoon dried thyme

Kosher salt and black pepper

1 to 2 tablespoons fresh lemon juice

For years, I have disliked the term "cauliflower steaks." But to be honest, calling these "cauliflower slabs" or "cauliflower hunks" just didn't sound as good.

Because they really are a slab, a steak, a big old hunk of cauliflower. A hunk that is roasted to perfection, with crispy golden edges and caramelized sides, which is cooked until it's so tender, your fork slides in like butter.

And then they are topped with marinated goat cheese. And the goat cheese melts slightly because the cauliflower slabs are still warm and, oh my, it's like a religious experience. A very vegetable-y religious experience. And a delicious one, too!

Preheat the oven to 425°F.

Slice the cauliflower head into large slabs or simply break it into florets. Place it on a baking sheet. Drizzle with the olive oil. Season with the salt, pepper, and red pepper flakes.

Roast the cauliflower for 20 to 25 minutes, until golden brown and toasty. Gently flip it once during cook time.

make the herby goat cheese   While the cauliflower roasts, place the goat cheese in the bowl of a food processor. Blend until it's completely creamy and whipped, scraping down the sides as needed.

Add the olive oil, chives, rosemary, thyme, a big pinch of salt and pepper, and 1 tablespoon of the lemon juice. Add more lemon juice as needed for flavor or thinning out. Transfer the mixture to a bowl.

When the cauliflower is done, drizzle it all over with the goat cheese. Top with the pistachios and a sprinkling of chives. Serve!

10-Minute Meal Prep

The herby goat cheese can be made ahead of time and stored in the fridge. I do like it at room temperature to serve.

spaghetti squash bolognese

2 spaghetti squash, sliced in half lengthwise

2 tablespoons extra-virgin olive oil

Kosher salt and black pepper

1 medium sweet onion, diced

4 garlic cloves, minced

8 ounces cremini mushrooms, chopped

1 pound lean ground turkey or beef

2 tablespoons tomato paste

½ teaspoon dried basil

½ teaspoon dried oregano

¼ teaspoon crushed red pepper flakes

1 tablespoon brown sugar

½ cup dry red wine

28 ounces crushed fire roasted tomatoes

½ cup freshly grated Parmesan cheese, plus more for serving

1 cup freshly grated provolone cheese

Chopped fresh basil, for serving

10-Minute Meal Prep

The Bolognese can be made ahead of time and stored in the fridge until ready to use. The squash can be sliced and roasted ahead of time, then stored in the fridge for 1 to 2 days until ready to use. When assembled, it may take a bit longer in the oven to warm if it is cold.

Spaghetti squash is one of my go-to meals in the winter. The kids LOVE it, if only because the roasted strands are super fun to twirl on a fork. And I love it because it's so easy to make and requires little hands-on time.

My favorite way to make this is with leftover Bolognese. So, if I've served Bolognese in a traditional way a day or two before, I will use it as leftovers here!

This is also fun to make and serve because everyone gets their own little portion. A little spaghetti squash bowl. Personal-pan spaghetti squashes!

Okay, you get the point. These are saucy, cheesy, and oh-so-good.

Preheat the oven to 425°F. Line a baking sheet with foil and spray with nonstick spray.

Slice the spaghetti squash in half lengthwise and scrape out the seeds. Brush the cut sides with 1 tablespoon of the olive oil. Place the squash cut-side down on the baking sheet. Roast for 25 minutes, until the squash is fork-tender. While the squash is roasting, make the Bolognese.

Heat the remaining 1 tablespoon of olive oil in a large pot over medium heat. Add the onion, along with a pinch of salt and pepper, and cook, stirring occasionally, until softened, 5 to 6 minutes. Add the garlic and mushrooms. Stir and cook for another 5 or 6 minutes, until the mushrooms soften.

Add the turkey and break it apart with a wooden spoon. Brown it, stirring and breaking it apart, until it's cooked through, 6 to 8 minutes. Stir in the tomato paste, basil, oregano, red pepper flakes, and brown sugar. Cook for 2 more minutes.

Add the wine, tomatoes, and Parmesan. Bring the mixture to a boil, then reduce to a simmer and cover, cooking for 15 minutes (or even longer if you wish!).

Remove the baking sheet from the oven and flip over the squash. Use a fork to scrape the squash strands from the side. This should happen easily because they are tender. I like to scrape most of the squash inside the skin so it is easier to eat when topped with the Bolognese. It also makes it easier to season. Season the squash with salt and pepper.

Scoop some of the Bolognese directly into the squash. I use anywhere from ⅔ to ¾ cup, depending on the size of the squash. (Extra Bolognese can be stored in the fridge for 4 to 5 days or even in the freezer for up to 3 months.) Top with the provolone cheese. Stick the squash back in the oven for about 10 more minutes, so the cheese melts and everything can come together.

Remove and sprinkle with Parmesan and basil before serving!

black bean turkey chili with green chile cornbread muffins

2 tablespoons extra-virgin olive oil

1 large sweet onion, diced

1 red bell pepper, diced

4 garlic cloves, minced

Kosher salt and black pepper

1 pound ground turkey

1 tablespoon tomato paste

2 tablespoons chili powder

1 tablespoon smoked paprika

1 teaspoon cumin

1 teaspoon onion powder

½ teaspoon crushed red pepper flakes

2 (14-ounce) cans black beans, drained and rinsed

14 ounces crushed fire roasted tomatoes

¾ to 1 cup chicken stock (see page 113)

1 tablespoon maple syrup

I make black bean turkey chili when I need something quick. It's also a recipe I love to make ahead of time for both dinners and lunches, and one that everyone goes completely wild over!

I make it on Halloween night or for a family party and serve it with a giant chili bar—toppings galore. Double or even triple batches of this chili are great, and it freezes so well, too.

Like most chilis, the flavor gets better as it sits.

I also like to make these little green chile cornbread poppers to serve with the chili. They are Eddie's favorite. I will dip them or even crumble them over the soup. He eats them with just about any meal and even loves them with strawberry jam on top.

Heat the olive oil in a large stockpot over medium heat. Add the onion, pepper, and garlic with a big pinch of salt and pepper. Cook, stirring often, until the vegetables soften, 5 to 6 minutes.

Add the ground turkey. I push the vegetables to the side so the meat can brown nicely. Break it apart into crumbles and cook until it's cooked through, 8 to 10 minutes.

Stir in the tomato paste and cook for 3 minutes. Stir in the chili powder, paprika, cumin, onion powder, and red pepper flakes. Cook for another 3 minutes, stirring occasionally.

Add the black beans, tomatoes, chicken stock, and maple syrup. Bring the mixture to a boil, then reduce it to a simmer and cover the pot. Simmer for at least 20 minutes (or as long as you wish!), then serve.

10-Minute Meal Prep

The chili ingredients can be measured and chopped ahead of time and stored in the fridge if needed. The cornbread can be baked ahead of time.

green chile cornbread muffins

1¼ cups all-purpose flour

1½ cups finely ground cornmeal

1 tablespoon baking powder

1 teaspoon kosher salt

⅔ cup sugar

4 large eggs, lightly beaten

¾ cup (1½ sticks) unsalted butter, melted and cooled

⅓ cup plain Greek yogurt or sour cream

4 ounces diced mild green chiles

½ cup corn (fresh or frozen is fine)

make the green chile cornbread muffins   I make these muffins while the chili is cooking. Preheat the oven to 350°F. Line a twelve-cup muffin tin with liners.

In a large bowl, whisk together the flour, cornmeal, baking powder, and salt.

In another large bowl, whisk together the sugar and the eggs. Whisk in the melted butter. Whisk in the yogurt.

Mix the dry ingredients into the wet ingredients until just combined. Stir in the green chiles and corn. Fill the muffin cups three-quarters of the way full.

Bake for 25 to 30 minutes, or until the center is set and the top is golden. Serve with the chili.

crispy chicken with broccoli slaw

1 pound boneless, skinless chicken breasts

Kosher salt and black pepper

2 large eggs, lightly beaten

1½ cups seasoned bread crumbs

⅔ cup finely grated Parmesan cheese

3 to 4 tablespoons extra-virgin olive oil

broccoli slaw

12 ounces packaged broccoli slaw

6 scallions, thinly sliced

⅔ cup toasted sunflower seeds

1 tablespoon toasted sesame seeds

½ cup avocado, canola, or other neutral oil

⅓ cup rice wine vinegar

¼ cup toasted sesame oil

¼ cup honey

1 tablespoon fresh lime juice

Kosher salt and black pepper

10-Minute Meal Prep

All the ingredients can be measured out and stored in the fridge as needed. The broccoli slaw can also be fully made ahead of time—it's great after it sits in the fridge for a day.

As we learned in the lunch chapter (page 81), I love using slaw as a salad base. There is just so much texture in slaw that you can't find anywhere else. It's fun to eat! It's crunchy and satisfying, and you can shred a bunch of different ingredients to make it super special and different each time.

For this recipe I love to use broccoli slaw. These days, it's pretty common to find broccoli slaw in your local grocery store. It will be by the coleslaw or the bagged broccoli, and I always have a bag or two on hand for easy lunches and dinners.

There are many different ways that I like to boost the slaw, whether it's by adding extra cabbage or kale, some dried fruit and nuts, and of course, my own dressing. That works as the base, and then I make a crispy chicken cutlet for the top, slicing it as thinly as possible. Oh my gosh—this is so crunchy and crispy. My kids go wild! It's a surefire way to get them to eat salad.

The slaw is hearty enough for a vinaigrette or a creamy dressing, and it's very forgiving. Use whatever dressing you love, along with other toppings if you wish.

My method for the chicken cutlets is also the way I make all our crispy chicken. You can serve the chicken with other sides from this chapter, such as the herby smashed potatoes (page 141) or lemon rice (page 118). It's so wonderful.

Thinly slice the chicken breasts lengthwise to make thin chicken cutlets. You want THIN slices—ones you can almost see through! I get three to four thin slices from one chicken breast. Season the chicken all over with salt and pepper. Line a baking sheet with paper towels.

Place the whisked eggs in a shallow plate or bowl. Stir together the bread crumbs and Parmesan in another plate or bowl.

Heat 1 to 2 tablespoons of olive oil in a large skillet over medium heat. I like to heat the oil for a good 5 minutes before adding the chicken. Watch the heat the entire time—if the oil seems to be too hot or starts smoking, make sure to lower the heat!

Dip each piece of chicken in the egg, then in the bread crumbs, pressing gently so the crumbs adhere.

Add the chicken to the skillet two or three pieces at a time. Cook on each side until deeply golden, 3 to 4 minutes per side. This should cook the chicken the entire way through, but check the temperature to make sure it is 165°F inside if you're unsure. Remove each piece of chicken and place it on the paper towel–lined sheet. Repeat with the remaining oil and chicken.

make the broccoli slaw   Place the broccoli slaw in a bowl. Add the scallions and the sunflower seeds. Sprinkle in the sesame seeds.

Place the neutral oil, vinegar, sesame oil, honey, and lime juice in a blender or bowl with a big pinch of salt and pepper. Blend or whisk together until smooth and combined. Pour half of the dressing over the broccoli slaw and toss it together well. Refrigerate for 30 minutes before serving. Use the remaining dressing for serving the final dish, adding as much more as you'd like.

easy parmesan chickpea soup with spinach

1 tablespoon extra-virgin olive oil

½ medium sweet onion, diced

4 garlic cloves, minced

Kosher salt and black pepper

Pinch of crushed red pepper flakes

1 or 2 (14-ounce) cans chickpeas, drained and rinsed

1 Parmesan rind, about 1 inch in size

4 cups chicken or vegetable stock

¾ cup tiny-cut pasta, like pastina, ditalini, or farfalline

5 ounces frozen spinach or 8 ounces fresh spinach

Freshly grated Parmesan cheese, for serving

Lemon wedges, for serving

This soup is embarrassingly easy and incredibly comforting. The key is the Parmesan broth!

Adding a Parmesan rind to the broth brings in such a fabulous rich and cheesy flavor. I have Parmesan rinds on hand at all times for this exact reason. They add something special to soups and stews. And in this case, they flavor the broth in a savory, salty way that you can't achieve from anything else.

This soup is made with a tiny cut of pasta, some spinach (both fresh and frozen work), and a can or two of chickpeas (depending on how hearty you like your soup). The recipe comes together SO quickly and is soul-warming and satisfying, while being incredibly easy. Add a salad or even a few slices of sourdough to this meal and you will be completely satisfied. It's cozy comfort food that brings warmth from the inside out.

Heat the olive oil in a large pot over medium-low heat. Stir in the onion and garlic with a big pinch of salt and pepper. Cook for about 5 minutes, until the onion is translucent. Stir in the red pepper flakes.

Stir in the chickpeas, Parmesan rind, and stock. Bring the mixture to a boil. Once boiling, add your pasta. Cook the pasta until al dente according to package instructions, somewhere between 8 and 12 minutes.

Once the pasta is cooked, stir in the spinach. Taste and season with extra salt and pepper. Top with lots of Parmesan. Ladle into bowls and serve with lemon wedges.

10-Minute Meal Prep

The onion can be chopped ahead of time and stored in the fridge.

crispy lemon chicken kale caesar salad

1 pound boneless, skinless chicken breasts

Kosher salt and black pepper

2 large eggs, lightly beaten

1½ cups seasoned bread crumbs

⅔ cup finely grated Parmesan cheese

3 teaspoons freshly grated lemon zest

3 to 4 tablespoons extra-virgin olive oil, plus ½ tablespoon more for the kale

6 to 8 cups chopped Tuscan kale

1 batch Lemon Caesar Dressing (page 34)

½ cup shaved Parmesan cheese

Another version of the thin and crispy chicken that we love involves lemon. Surprise, surprise!

For this chicken, I add some freshly grated lemon zest right to the cheese and bread crumb mixture. I also use my lemon Caesar dressing for this, making it a bright and refreshing dish all around. It's filled with so much flavor, texture, and crunch that no one can resist.

Thinly slice the chicken breasts lengthwise to make thin chicken cutlets. You want THIN slices—ones you can almost see through! I get three to four thin slices from one chicken breast. Season the chicken all over with salt and pepper. Line a baking sheet with paper towels.

Place the whisked eggs in a shallow plate or bowl. Stir together the bread crumbs, lemon zest, and Parmesan in another plate or bowl.

Heat 1 to 2 tablespoons of olive oil in a large skillet over medium heat. I like to heat the oil for a good 5 minutes before adding the chicken. Watch the heat the entire time—if the oil seems to be too hot or starts smoking, make sure to lower the heat!

Dip each piece of chicken in the egg, then in the bread crumbs, pressing gently so the crumbs adhere.

Add the chicken to the skillet two or three pieces at a time. Cook on each side until deeply golden, 3 to 4 minutes per side. This should cook the chicken the entire way through but check the temperature to make sure it is 165°F inside if you're unsure. Remove each piece of chicken and place it on the paper towel–lined sheet. Repeat with the remaining chicken.

Place the kale in a large bowl. Add ½ tablespoon of olive oil and massage the kale well with your hands. Let sit for 5 minutes. Add the Caesar dressing to the kale and toss well.

Slice the chicken into thin strips. Place it in the salad. Top with the shaved Parmesan. Serve!

10-Minute Meal Prep

The bread crumb mixture can be stirred together and stored in the fridge until ready to use. The kale can be cleaned, chopped, and stored in the fridge until ready to use. The dressing can also be made ahead of time.

flank steak with garlicky sautéed kale

garlicky kale

1 large bunch of kale, stems removed

2 to 3 tablespoons extra-virgin olive oil

8 garlic cloves, thinly sliced

½ teaspoon crushed red pepper flakes

Kosher salt and black pepper

½ teaspoon fresh lemon zest

2 tablespoons fresh lemon juice

steak

1 tablespoon brown sugar

1 teaspoon kosher salt

1 teaspoon black pepper

1 teaspoon instant espresso powder

½ teaspoon garlic powder

½ teaspoon smoked paprika

2 (6-ounce) flank steaks

2 to 3 tablespoons unsalted butter

10-Minute Meal Prep

The kale can be washed and dried, then stored in the fridge until ready to use. I store mine in a resealable bag with a paper towel. The spices for the steak can be mixed and stored together ahead of time.

We don't eat a ton of red meat, but when we do, I like to serve it with this kale.

If you think you don't like kale, you have got to try it this way. Think lots of freshly chopped garlic, crushed red pepper flakes, lemon zest and juice, olive oil, salt, and pepper. Simple and basic ingredients but ones that make the world go 'round.

Bring out the steaks 30 minutes before cook time. When everything is sautéed together, the kale loses its bitterness and takes on the flavor of the garlic and lemon. It is such a great complement to the steak that also melts in your mouth. And it's a fabulous side dish to have in your recipe box.

I make this kale often with other dishes—ones that are lacking a vegetable, or when I want to make a recipe that doesn't require turning on the oven because this one is made strictly on the stovetop.

I could eat a whole head of kale this way!

make the garlicky kale   I start the kale before the steak because it can hang out in the pan while the steak cooks and rests. Clean the kale, pat it dry, and tear or chop into pieces.

Heat the olive oil in a large saucepan or Dutch oven over medium heat. Add the garlic and red pepper flakes. Cook for 1 minute. Stir in the kale. Add a big pinch of salt and pepper. Cook, stirring often, until the kale wilts, 5 to 6 minutes.

Stir in the lemon zest and juice. Taste and season additionally if needed.

make the steak   Preheat the oven to 400°F.

In a bowl, stir together the brown sugar, salt, pepper, espresso powder, garlic powder, and paprika. Cover the steaks all over with the rub.

Melt the butter in a cast-iron skillet over medium-high heat. Once melted, add the steaks and cook on both sides until deeply seared, 2 to 3 minutes per side. Once seared, immediately transfer the steaks to the oven for 5 to 8 minutes, or until it reaches the desired doneness.

Let the steaks rest for 5 to 10 minutes before slicing. Serve with the kale.

chicken tortellini soup with fire roasted tomatoes

1 tablespoon extra-virgin olive oil

1 medium sweet onion, diced

4 garlic cloves, minced

Kosher salt and black pepper

1 tablespoon tomato paste

28 ounces crushed fire roasted tomatoes

1½ cups cooked, shredded chicken

1 Parmesan rind, about 1 inch in size

4 to 5 cups chicken stock (see page 113)

¾ cup heavy cream

4 cups chopped kale

8 to 12 ounces cheese tortellini

Grated Parmesan cheese, for serving

Crushed red pepper flakes, for serving

Tortellini is my first choice of pasta when it comes to soup. I love how filling it makes the soup—it almost tastes like a pasta dish! It also allows for so much versatility in soup. There can be meat or no meat, added beans, or other vegetables.

The secret ingredient here is fire roasted tomatoes. I use fire roasted tomatoes whenever possible, and I simmer them until they break down. The flavor is smoky and unique, and more complicated than regular tomatoes. It makes a huge difference in recipes and really improves flavors.

I also add some cream in this soup. It works wonders for added satiety. Plus, then it's like a creamy tomato soup, with tortellini. Your spoon won't be able to stay out of it!

P.S. You can sub in one or two cans of white beans or chickpeas for the chicken to make this a veg-based soup.

Heat the olive oil in a large stockpot over medium-low heat. Stir in the onion, garlic, and a big pinch of salt and pepper. Cook, stirring often, until the onion softens, 5 to 6 minutes.

Stir in the tomato paste. Cook for a few minutes, allowing the color (and flavor!) to deepen. Pour in the crushed tomatoes, chicken, Parmesan rind, and 4 cups of the chicken stock. Bring the mixture to a boil. Reduce it to a simmer and cover, then simmer for 15 to 20 minutes.

After 20 minutes, stir in the heavy cream, then the kale. Stir in the tortellini and cook for about 5 minutes, until it's tender and cooked through. This is the time to decide if you want to add the remaining cup of chicken stock. If so, add it in! Remember that the tortellini will soak up the liquid as it sits.

Taste the soup and season with additional salt and pepper if needed.

Serve immediately, sprinkled with Parmesan and red pepper flakes.

10-Minute Meal Prep

The chicken can be cooked and shredded ahead of time, or pulled off a rotisserie chicken and stored in the fridge. The entire soup base can even be made ahead of time, and then reheated for cooking the tortellini!

french onion dutch baby

caramelized onions

3 tablespoons unsalted butter

3 large sweet onions

Kosher salt

½ teaspoon baking soda

dutch baby

5 tablespoons unsalted butter

6 large eggs

1 cup whole milk

½ teaspoon kosher salt

½ teaspoon dried thyme

1 cup all-purpose flour

1 cup freshly grated Gruyère cheese

Thyme sprigs, for serving

We love a good Dutch baby—the big German puffed pancake that can feed a crowd. And the only thing I love more than a Dutch baby? A savory Dutch baby!

I also have this thing where I want to add caramelized onions to everything. I "French onion" things, technically. Caramelized onions, Gruyère, thyme—all the friends join in. These three ingredients make anything taste delicious, so I knew they'd be the perfect combo of flavors for a big, savory pancake that can be served for brunch or dinner.

Caramelizing the onions takes some time, and it can be a pain. You won't get good, caramelized onions on their own in less than an hour, but I'm using a hack here by adding some baking soda to speed up the process. Recipes calling for caramelized onions are a game changer!

This is one of those special, indulgent dishes you make for a holiday meal. Don't be alarmed at how much the pancake puffs up! The base of the pancake is made with Gruyère and thyme, topped with the onions, and served with extra herbs. It's so decadent and filling, made with a flavor profile that you can't help but remember.

make the onions Heat the butter in an oven-safe 12-inch pan over medium heat. Add the onions and a big pinch of salt. Cook, stirring occasionally, for about 15 minutes, until the onions are soft. Reduce the heat to medium-low, add the baking soda, and cook for another 15 minutes or so, stirring often, until caramelized.

While the onions are caramelizing, preheat the oven to 425°F.

Transfer the onions from the skillet to a plate and set aside.

make the dutch baby Place the butter in the same oven-safe skillet you used for the onions. Stick it in the oven and let the butter melt. If it starts to brown, that's good, too!

In a blender, combine the eggs, milk, salt, thyme, and flour. Blend until smooth and well combined. Open the lid of the blender and, using a wooden spoon, stir in half of the caramelized onions and half of the Gruyère.

Remove the pan from the oven and pour the mixture directly into the pan. Return the pan to the oven and bake for about 25 minutes, until the pancake is puffed up and golden.

Remove and immediately sprinkle with the remaining Gruyère. Top with the leftover caramelized onions. Garnish with fresh thyme. Slice and serve.

10-Minute Meal Prep

The onions can be caramelized ahead of time and stored in the fridge. Bring them to room temperature before using. The cheese can also be grated ahead of time.

cilantro lime sheet pan shrimp fajitas

2 bell peppers (red, orange, or yellow), thinly sliced

1 medium sweet onion, thinly sliced

1 batch Cilantro Lime Dressing (page 29)

1 pound raw, peeled, deveined shrimp

Warm tortillas, for serving

Cotija cheese, for serving

Quick Pickled Onions (page 40), for serving (optional)

¼ cup chopped fresh cilantro, for serving (optional)

Lime wedges, for serving

In another installment of the "I love my cilantro lime dressing" chronicles, I bring you . . . shrimp fajitas! These shrimp fajitas are made on a sheet pan and are super easy, perfect for taco night, and great for leftovers.

Like my other sheet pan meals, I add the vegetables and shrimp in increments. I toast some corn tortillas, add a sprinkling of cotija cheese, and have these light, lovely, satisfying, and delicious fajitas.

We all go wild for them!

Preheat the oven to 425°F.

Place the peppers and onion on a baking sheet. Add half of the cilantro lime dressing and toss them well until they're evenly coated. Stick the baking sheet in the oven and roast for 15 to 20 minutes, tossing once or twice during cooking.

In the meantime, place the shrimp in a bowl and pour the remaining marinade over the top. Let sit until the peppers and onion are roasted.

Once the vegetables are done, toss them a few times and scoop them over to one side of the pan. Place the shrimp on the sheet in a single layer. Roast the shrimp for 6 to 8 minutes, or until they're just pink and opaque.

When the shrimp are finished, assemble your fajitas! Start with the peppers and onion on the tortillas, then add on the shrimp. Sprinkle with cotija cheese and top with pickled onions and the fresh cilantro if you wish. Serve with lime wedges for squeezing.

10-Minute Meal Prep

The cilantro lime dressing can be made ahead of time. The peppers and onion can be sliced and stored in the fridge until ready to use.

weeknight white pizza

1 sheet of puff pastry, thawed if frozen

2 tablespoons extra-virgin olive oil

4 garlic cloves, minced

Pinch of crushed red pepper flakes

2 Roma or beefsteak tomatoes, thinly sliced

Kosher salt and black pepper

8 ounces freshly grated provolone or mozzarella cheese, or an Italian blend

2 ounces freshly grated Parmesan cheese, plus more for serving

½ teaspoon dried basil

When you're in a time pinch, this pizza is possibly the best way to use puff pastry. Just add cheese. Add tomatoes. More cheese. Olive oil. Herbs. Bake until golden and puffed and cheesy and it smells like you've lit a pizza margherita candle in your kitchen. You win at dinner.

Preheat the oven to 425°F. Line a baking sheet with parchment paper and place the sheet of puff pastry on top. Poke it all over with a fork (this prevents big bubbles!) and set aside.

Heat the olive oil in a skillet over low heat. Stir in the garlic and red pepper flakes. Cook for 1 to 2 minutes, until the garlic is sizzling. Let it cool slightly.

While the seasoned oil is cooling, place the tomato slices on a paper towel and sprinkle all over with salt. Let sit for 10 minutes, then pat dry with a paper towel.

Brush the puff pastry all over with the garlic oil. Sprinkle all over with the cheeses, leaving a 1-inch border around the edges. Top with the tomato slices. Sprinkle on some pepper and the basil. Drizzle a bit more garlic oil on (just a bit!) and sprinkle with more Parmesan.

Bake for 20 to 25 minutes, until golden and puffed and cheesy! Remove from the oven and let cool for 5 minutes. Sprinkle with additional Parmesan, slice, and serve!

10-Minute Meal Prep

The cheese can be grated ahead of time and stored in the fridge.

cast-iron skillet pepperoni pizza with tomato jam

pizza dough

½ cup warm water

2 teaspoons active dry yeast

½ tablespoon honey

1 tablespoon extra-virgin olive oil, plus 1 tablespoon for the pan and extra for the bowl

1¾ cups all-purpose flour, plus extra for kneading and dusting

1 teaspoon kosher salt

Coarse cornmeal for dusting (optional)

pizza toppings

8 ounces torn fresh mozzarella cheese

15 pepperoni slices

⅓ cup Quick Tomato Jam (page 43)

4 garlic cloves, minced

Chopped fresh chives or scallions, for serving

Grated Parmesan cheese

Hot honey, for serving

10-Minute Meal Prep

The dough can be made ahead of time and put in the fridge after rising. The cheeses and tomato jam can be prepared ahead of time, too.

We make homemade pizza quite frequently. Pizza is probably everyone's favorite in the house. We make large pizzas, single-serving pizzas, classic versions, or ones with wacky toppings. This is a mix of all those kinds. Spicy pepperoni and sweet tomato jam go on this pizza, for the ultimate cheesy, savory but sweet bite.

And the method here, of making the pizza in a cast-iron skillet, is the closest I've found to real wood-fired pizza.

In a large bowl, combine the water, yeast, honey, and olive oil. Mix with a spoon, then let sit until foamy, about 10 minutes. Add the flour and salt, stirring with a spoon until the dough comes together but is still sticky. Knead with your hands, adding additional flour until it's not sticky, but silky and smooth. Rub the same bowl with olive oil, then place the dough inside, turning to coat. Cover with a towel and place in a warm place to rise for 1 to 1½ hours.

At this point, I get my toppings ready. I have my cheese grated, the pepperoni out, and the jam prepared.

Heat a 10- or 12-inch cast-iron pan over medium heat. I like to heat mine for a full 5 to 10 minutes before placing the dough in it. At the same time, preheat the broiler in your oven to the high setting. Make sure the oven rack is in the center and not directly below the broiler.

After the dough has risen, punch it down and place it back on a floured surface.

Using a rolling pin or your hands, form it loosely into a circle that fits in your cast-iron pan.

Add 1 tablespoon of olive oil to the preheated pan and make sure it coats the bottom of the pan. Place your dough in the pan. Cook for 1 to 2 minutes, until the dough is bubbling up. Carefully and quickly, spread the tomato jam on top of the dough, leaving a border for the crust. Sprinkle with the garlic and mozzarella. Add the pepperoni.

Place the skillet in the middle of the oven with the broiler on. Broil for about 5 minutes—but watch it! It can burn fast. I find that my pizza can take between 5 and 10 minutes, so just keep an eye on it until it is as golden and bubbly as you'd like.

Remove the pan and let the pizza cool for a few minutes. Sprinkle with the chives or scallions and lots of Parmesan and drizzle with hot honey. Slice and serve!

CHAPTER 5

easy
entertaining
& snacks

This one is also known as the chapter dedicated to how much I love cheese. I love it. A lot.

Having people over to our home, whether it's a planned gathering or a spur-of-the-moment drop-by is one of my favorite things. I love entertaining friends and family, having some great snacks and good conversation, and doing so in a stress-free manner.

Eddie once gave me the biggest compliment of all. He said he couldn't believe how calmly and quickly I could throw together a small party, complete with good food. He said I make it look effortless, and as you know by now, that is one of my main goals when it comes to meals!

I never want my guests to feel any of the stress I have around entertaining, so I try to keep things as simple as possible. First, I always make sure to prepare snacks or meals that don't require me standing over the stove, hiding away in the kitchen. I want to enjoy my company and spend time with

them. Because of that, most of the snacks you'll find in this chapter are things that you can make ahead of time. Many are simple and pretty, while providing a showstopping punch of flavor. That's why they're my favorites. Everyone loves them!

From my Ricotta Jam Jar (my own twist on the famous Nordstrom cafe recipe; page 177) to Green Chile Chilled Queso (unique and incredible; page 190) to Pomegranate Pepita Guacamole (page 185), all of these hit the spot. They are crowd-pleasers and perfect for your next gathering, or just a night when you want to have a snack dinner.

Snack dinner. The best kind!

P.S. I wasn't joking about the amount of cheese in this chapter. But the good news is that you can leave it out of a few recipes (the guac, the fritters) without issue! ●

ricotta jam jar

1 baguette, thinly sliced

3 tablespoons extra-virgin olive oil

Several pinches of sea salt

Garlic powder

½ cup ricotta cheese

⅓ cup Our All-Time Favorite Basil Pesto (page 35)

⅓ cup Quick Tomato Jam (page 43)

Handful of fresh herbs, like basil or oregano, chopped, for serving

I have been making the ricotta jam jar for years, and it is always a huge hit at parties.

It's beautiful. It looks impressive, but it's super easy. It can be fully made ahead of time, which is key. And it works for a party or even just as a dinner appetizer.

This is a versatile recipe that layers creamy ricotta cheese with my tomato jam and basil pesto. The magic is in the presentation itself. And while I tend to have individually wrapped cubes of my homemade pesto in the freezer, even through winter, you can always use your favorite jarred pesto in a pinch.

Preheat the oven to 400°F. Place the baguette slices on a baking sheet. Drizzle the bread with the olive oil and sprinkle with the salt and garlic powder. Bake for 10 to 12 minutes, until golden and crunchy.

While the baguette is toasting, place the ricotta cheese in a food processor and blend until creamy and smooth. Scoop it into an 8-ounce jar.

Add the pesto on top. Add the tomato jam on top of the pesto. Sprinkle with the fresh herbs. Serve with the toasts.

10-Minute Meal Prep

The pesto and tomato jam can both be made ahead of time and stored in the fridge. The baguette can also be sliced and toasted ahead of time.

gouda fonduta

1 pound Gouda cheese, cut into cubes

8 ounces fontina cheese, cut into cubes

1 tablespoon chopped fresh rosemary

1 tablespoon chopped fresh chives

1 teaspoon chopped fresh thyme

1 tablespoon extra-virgin olive oil

Crackers, crudité, or baguette slices, for serving

Gouda fonduta. I couldn't resist rhyming!

This melty, cheesy dip reminds me of the fondue that my mom would make us on New Year's Eve when I was kid. She made the classic Gruyère- and Emmentaler-focused cheese fondue, and even today, the taste and smell takes me right back to childhood.

However, Gouda is a little more forgiving for those picky eaters, and the nutty sharpness is incredibly flavorful.

And we're skipping the traditional fondue method for a very easy one: Chop your cheese into chunks, add some herbs, and throw the whole thing in the oven.

The end result is a pot of melted cheese that no baguette can resist.

Preheat the broiler in your oven to high.

Place the Gouda and fontina cheeses in a baking dish or pie plate. Sprinkle the herbs all around it. Drizzle with the olive oil.

Place the dish on the oven rack directly under the broiler. Broil until the cheese is melted, 5 to 6 minutes. (This will vary greatly depending on your broiler! Keep an eye on the cheese the entire time and check it every 2 minutes.)

Remove and serve with crackers, crudité, or baguette slices.

10-Minute Meal Prep

The cheese can be cut into cubes ahead of time and stored in the fridge.

chili cantaloupe wedges

1 cantalolupe, seeded and sliced into 12 wedges

12 slices prosciutto

3 to 4 tablespoons chili oil

3 tablespoons chopped fresh chives

2 tablespoons chiffonade basil

Summer food is my favorite for entertaining because it's just so beautiful. Vibrant, fresh, juicy, and inviting. Who can say no?

These cantaloupe wedges can be thrown together in a matter of minutes, or even prepped ahead of a party. They look beautiful on a platter all while being fun (and easy!) to eat. The sweet-and-savory combo surprises everyone, and these are lovely and satisfying.

They also make a pretty lunch plate for yourself, too.

Remove the rind from the outside of the cantaloupe wedges.

Wrap a slice of prosciutto around the wedge. Repeat with the remaining cantaloupe wedges and prosciutto slices.

Drizzle with the chili oil. Sprinkle with the chives and fresh basil. Serve!

10-Minute Meal Prep

The cantaloupe can be sliced into wedges and stored in the fridge ahead of time.

our favorite marinated cheese

8 ounces sharp Cheddar cheese, cut into cubes

4 ounces fontina cheese, cut into pieces

4 ounces goat cheese, cut into pieces

1 (14-ounce) jar roasted red peppers in oil, peppers chopped and oil reserved

¼ to ⅓ cup extra-virgin olive oil

½ cup red wine vinegar

2 teaspoons honey

½ teaspoon dried basil

½ teaspoon dried oregano

¼ teaspoon kosher salt

¼ teaspoon freshly cracked black pepper

2 scallions, thinly sliced

2 garlic cloves, minced

3 tablespoons chopped fresh basil

2 tablespoons chopped fresh parsley

1 tablespoon chopped fresh dill

Crackers or baguette slices, for serving

Marinated cheese. Oh let me count the ways in which I love you. When I say that people lose their marbles over this recipe, I mean it. It gets gobbled up at parties. The earlier you make it, the better, because the flavors marry, and you end up shocked at how incredible these everyday ingredients taste when combined.

This is another recipe that looks festive and is especially perfect for the holiday season. There is no better way to celebrate cheese!

Place the Cheddar, fontina, and goat cheese in a large serving dish or pie plate that has a lip—something that allows you to cover it in the marinade. Alternate the pieces so the goat cheese is distributed throughout the dish.

In a bowl, whisk together the oil from the jar of roasted red peppers, the olive oil, vinegar, honey, dried basil, oregano, salt, pepper, scallions, garlic, fresh basil, parsley, and dill. Stir in the roasted red peppers.

Pour the marinade over the cheese. Refrigerate for at least 4 hours, or overnight. Serve with crackers or baguette slices.

10-Minute Meal Prep

The cheeses can be cut and stored in the fridge until ready to use. The dressing can be mixed up a few hours before pouring it over the cheese.

cheesy double pesto twists

2 sheets frozen puff pastry, thawed

½ cup Sun-Dried Tomato Pesto
(page 34)

½ cup Our All-Time Favorite Basil
Pesto (page 35)

1 cup freshly shredded mozzarella
cheese

1 egg + 1 teaspoon water, lightly
beaten, for egg wash

¼ cup finely grated Parmesan,
plus extra for serving

Chopped fresh herbs, for serving
(optional)

Here we have another use for my favorite ingredient, puff pastry.

These twists look beautiful and impressive, but it's really very simple. I've seen these made with all sorts of dips, cheeses, and spreads, but I've never encountered a dual pesto version.

This is a snack best made when you have leftover pesto. If I want a festive app, I alternate my sun-dried tomato and basil pestos to create these cute red-and-green twists. A sprinkle of Parmesan adds some savory flavor, and the pastry is twirled until it looks ultra-fancy.

Make this the center of your cheeseboard or serve it alone with some fresh basil. Beauty!

Preheat the oven to 425°F. Line a baking sheet with parchment paper.

Prep your puff pastry. Using a pizza cutter, cut a large circle out of each puff pastry sheet, wasting as little as possible. Place both circles on the parchment paper.

Spoon the tomato pesto on four sections of one sheet of pastry. I spoon it in a 1-inch section on the top, the bottom, the right, and the left side. In the remaining areas, spoon the basil pesto. Leave a ½-inch border around the edges. Brush the edges with egg wash. Top the whole thing with the mozzarella cheese. Top with the other circle of puff pastry, so they line up perfectly on top of each other with the filling in the center. Press the edges together.

Use a biscuit cutter (or the rim of a glass) to press into the center, but don't cut through. Use a sharp knife to cut slits in the puff pastry circle about 1 inch apart—from the center out to the edge. Take each of those slices and gently twist it from the center. Twist it two or three times. Don't worry if the filling is falling out and it looks messy—it will still bake up pretty!

Brush the pastry with the egg wash and sprinkle it with the Parmesan.

Bake on the center rack for 20 to 25 minutes, or until the puff pastry is golden and shiny. Serve immediately! Top with Parmesan, and fresh herbs if you wish.

10-Minute Meal Prep

The cheese can be shredded ahead of
time and stored in the fridge.

pomegranate pepita guacamole

4 ripe avocados

Kosher salt and black pepper

½ cup chopped fresh cilantro

3 tablespoons diced sweet onion

2 garlic cloves, minced

3 to 4 tablespoons freshly squeezed lime juice

½ cup pomegranate arils

½ cup roasted, salted pepitas

½ cup crumbled cotija cheese

Tortilla chips, for serving

Most days, I tend to be a guacamole purist. Give me some avocados, sweet onion, lime, cilantro, and jalapeño, plus lots of salt. A margarita on the side, of course. And I am a happy camper!

But in the event that I want to serve something special and "new"—you know, without totally reinventing an old favorite—this guacamole is my go-to. Just when I thought that guacamole couldn't get any better, we go and add pretty pops of pomegranate jewels. And now it's stunning!

The pepitas are salty and buttery, adding the perfect crunch. The pomegranate arils are gorgeous and juicy, adding a tart punch of sweetness.

In a large bowl, mash together the avocados with a big pinch of salt and pepper and the cilantro, onion, garlic, and 3 tablespoons of the lime juice. Taste and season with more salt or lime as needed. Stir in half of the pomegranate arils, the pepitas, and cotija cheese.

Scoop the guacamole in a bowl for serving. Top with the remaining pomegranate arils, pepitas, and cotija cheese. Serve with tortilla chips.

10-Minute Meal Prep

The ingredients can all be measured out ahead of time and stored in the fridge until ready to use.

grilled watermelon bruschetta

2 cups cherry tomatoes, halved or quartered

1 cup diced watermelon

8 garlic cloves, finely minced

Kosher salt and black pepper

2 tablespoons extra-virgin olive oil

1 to 2 tablespoons balsamic vinegar

¼ cup chiffonade basil

4 slices sourdough bread

It's a hot summer night and you don't want to turn on the oven. You're sitting on the patio with an ice-cold glass of sauvignon blanc, and you decide to chop up a bunch of your garden tomatoes, basil, and garlic. Throw some diced watermelon into the mix, adding that refreshing crunch and sweet flavor.

Sourdough bread is drizzled with olive oil and sprinkled with salt, then tossed on the grill for just a few minutes. You spoon that watermelon-tomato mixture over the golden toast and the bruschetta juice runs down the plate.

This is summer heaven. It's a lovely appetizer or snack or the perfect light lunch or dinner in the hot months. Refreshing, crunchy, satisfying, and oh-so-pretty.

Preheat your grill to the highest heat.

In a large bowl, combine the tomatoes, watermelon, minced garlic, and a big pinch of salt and pepper. Toss well. Drizzle in 1 tablespoon of the olive oil and 1 to 2 tablespoons of the balsamic vinegar. Toss again. Add the basil and toss.

Brush the bread slices with the remaining 1 tablespoon of olive oil. Place them directly on the grill. Grill for 1 to 2 minutes, until grill marks appear and the bread is toasted. Flip and grill for 1 to 2 minutes more.

Remove the bread from the grill and slice it in half. Top each piece with a heaping scoop of the bruschetta. Serve immediately!

10-Minute Meal Prep

The tomatoes and watermelon can be chopped ahead of time. The whole bruschetta topping can be made about 2 hours ahead of time and stored in the fridge.

buffalo cauliflower fritters

4 cups cauliflower florets

½ cup all-purpose flour

2 large eggs, lightly beaten

½ cup finely grated sharp
Cheddar cheese

½ cup crumbled blue cheese

3 tablespoons buffalo sauce,
plus more for serving

2 scallions, thinly sliced

3 tablespoons chopped fresh
cilantro

½ teaspoon garlic powder

¼ teaspoon kosher salt

¼ teaspoon black pepper

2 to 3 tablespoons olive oil,
for cooking

Chopped fresh chives, for serving

Yogurt Blue Cheese Sauce,
for serving (page 45)

My family loves buffalo chicken. Buffalo chicken anything and everything. And the only flavor I might love more? Buffalo cauliflower everything.

These adorable little bites are dragged through a Greek yogurt blue cheese sauce, which adds a refreshing coolness to the fritter.

These taste like fun bar food, made at home. They are so fantastic, a wonderful game-day snack or even a great dinner side dish.

Fill a skillet or saucepan with 1 inch of water and heat it over medium heat. Once simmering, add the cauliflower and cover the pan. Cook for 3 to 4 minutes, just until the cauliflower is slightly tender. Strain the cauliflower through a strainer.

Chop the cauliflower into small pieces. Mash half of the cauliflower pieces with a fork or potato masher.

In a large bowl, stir together the flour, eggs, cheeses, buffalo sauce, scallions, cilantro, garlic powder, salt, and pepper. Fold in the cauliflower.

Line a plate with paper towels. Heat a large nonstick skillet over medium heat. Add 1 tablespoon of the olive oil to start. Once the oil is hot, drop ½-cup scoops of the cauliflower mixture onto the pan. Cook for 2 to 3 minutes per side, until golden and crispy. Transfer the fritters to the paper towel–lined plate to remove excess grease. Repeat with remaining ingredients.

Serve with a sprinkling of chives, an extra drizzle of sauce, and a dollop of Yogurt Blue Cheese Sauce!

10-Minute Meal Prep

The cauliflower can be cooked ahead of time. The fritter mixture can also be mixed up and stored in the fridge a few hours ahead of time.

green chile chilled queso

1½ cups finely grated sharp Cheddar cheese

1½ cups finely grated Monterey Jack cheese

¾ cup mayonnaise

4 ounces mild diced green chiles

¼ cup thinly sliced scallions

3 tablespoons chopped cilantro

2 tablespoons diced pickled jalapeños

2 tablespoons freshly squeezed lime juice

Kosher salt and black pepper

Tortilla chips, crackers, pretzels, or veggies, for serving

I was skeptical about chilled queso, until I tried it. Much like pimento cheese, this spread is served cold, with grated cheese throughout it.

But don't underestimate it. It's delicious with tortilla chips, spread on a sandwich or cracker, or even topping a burger. It's melty in a chilled way—creamy and soft, but not served warm like fondue.

It works best if you make it a day ahead of time, because the flavors have time to sit and get acquainted. You won't be able to step away from the bowl!

Stir together the cheeses, mayo, chiles, scallions, cilantro, jalapeños, lime juice, and a big pinch of salt and pepper. Mix everything together until combined.

Cover and refrigerate for 2 hours (or overnight) before serving. This is great right out of the fridge, but I like to let it come to room temperature for 15 minutes or so before serving.

Serve with tortilla chips, crackers, pretzels, or veggies.

10-Minute Meal Prep

The cheese can be grated ahead of time and stored in the fridge.

chipotle caramel snack mix

½ cup (1 stick) unsalted butter

¼ cup light corn syrup

1 cup packed brown sugar

½ teaspoon chipotle chili powder

½ teaspoon smoked paprika

3 cups Rice Chex cereal

3 cups Corn Chex cereal

3 cups cheese crackers, such as Cheez-Its

2 cups mini pretzels

2 cups Cheerios

1 cup peanuts

1 cup cashews

This crunchy mix is one you can't keep your hands out of.

Sweet plus heat is the name of the game here, and this addictive snack blend is something you can make your own. Include your favorite ingredients. Give it as a holiday gift. Make it for a beach vacation snack.

You should probably make a double batch because the crowd will go wild.

Preheat the oven to 275°F. Line two baking sheets with parchment paper.

Place the butter, corn syrup, sugar, chili powder, and paprika in a microwave-safe bowl. Microwave in 30-second increments, stirring after each, until the butter is melted and the mixture combines. Stir it well so it looks caramelly.

Place the Chex cereals, crackers, pretzels, Cheerios, peanuts, and cashews in a large bowl. Pour the caramel mixture over the top and toss well to combine, even using your hands if needed. You want ALL pieces coated! This will take a good few minutes to coat everything.

Spread the mix on two baking sheets evenly. Bake for 1 hour, tossing well every 15 minutes so it toasts evenly. Remove from the oven and toss the mixture every 10 minutes or so until it cools so it doesn't all clump together. Store in a zip-top bag or sealed container.

10-Minute Meal Prep

The dry ingredients can be measured out and combined, then stored at room temperature until ready to use.

sizzled rosemary white bean dip

2 tablespoons extra-virgin olive oil

2 to 3 tablespoons coarsely chopped fresh rosemary

2 (14-ounce) cans cannellini beans, drained and rinsed

2 heads of Roasted Garlic (page 42)

Kosher salt and black pepper

1 tablespoon freshly squeezed lemon juice

3 to 4 tablespoons warm water

Vegetables, crackers, pita chips, or baguette slices, for serving

I can never get enough dip. Can you tell? This summer white bean dip is made by mashing creamy and buttery cannellini beans with fresh herbs, garlic, and a drizzle of olive oil. It's excellent served with vegetables, crackers, pita chips, or baguette slices, and it comes together super fast.

It's another make-ahead option. One that you can store in the fridge for a day or two until you're ready to use it. It's also something I love to make for the week ahead and use for lunch recipes. It can be a sandwich spread, a dip, or even a pizza sauce base.

Heat 1 tablespoon of the olive oil in a skillet over medium heat. Add the rosemary and cook for 1 to 2 minutes, just until it gets slightly golden and toasty. Remove from the heat. Reserve a spoonful of the rosemary off to the side.

To the bowl of a food processor, add the beans, the cloves from the roasted garlic, the olive oil from the pan with the rosemary, a big pinch of salt and pepper, and the lemon juice. Blend until the mixture is pureed and smooth. Drizzle in 2 to 3 tablespoons of the warm water with the processor running, adding more water until you reach your desired consistency. Taste and season with more salt and pepper as needed.

Spoon the dip into a bowl. Top with the remaining olive oil and the reserved rosemary. Serve with vegetables, crackers, pita chips, or baguette slices.

10-Minute Meal Prep

The beans can be drained and rinsed ahead of time and stored in the fridge.

roasted garlic feta dip

8 ounces feta cheese

1 head of Roasted Garlic (page 42)

4 tablespoons extra-virgin olive oil

Kosher salt and black pepper

1 tablespoon chopped fresh thyme

Pita chips, vegetables, or crackers, for serving

Years ago we had a local Greek restaurant that served the most incredible hot feta dip with roasted garlic. It was ridiculously creamy and smooth, and scooping up some with a soft, fluffy pita is still something I dream about today.

When the restaurant closed, I wanted to cry! How could I get that feta garlic dip now?

Challenge time: I had to make it myself.

This creamy dip is best served piping hot, with lots of pita triangles for dipping. But it's also wonderful spread inside a wrap or on a sandwich.

Preheat the oven to 400°F.

Place the feta cheese in the bowl of a food processor. Blend until the feta is creamy and smooth.

Transfer the feta to a small baking dish or pie plate. Top with the roasted garlic cloves (you can gently stir them in or leave them on top).

Drizzle with the olive oil, a pinch of salt and pepper, and the thyme.

Bake for about 20 minutes, until hot and melty. Serve with pita chips, vegetables, or crackers.

10-Minute Meal Prep

The feta can be whipped ahead of time and stored in the fridge.

treats, treats, treats

I won't lie. It was difficult to narrow down a few of my favorite desserts to share with you in this book. So, when I say that these are the best of the best, the ones I make the most often, you know it's the truth.

Here you'll find a slew of family favorites—desserts with fruit, ones loaded with chocolate, chewy cookies, and fluffy cakes.

I love serving dessert based on the season and the mood. Springtime might call for something lemony and light. A chilly snowy evening may call for warm cookies that can be dipped in hot chocolate. Summer means no-bake pies with buttery graham cracker crusts and treats you can make ahead of time and take to a cookout.

There is something here for everyone, and dessert is about sharing treats with those you love.

A little bite of something sweet is just what we all need. ●

spiced caramel honeycrisp apple galette

galette crust

2 cups sifted all-purpose flour

2 tablespoons granulated sugar

½ teaspoon cinnamon

½ teaspoon kosher salt

1 large egg, lightly beaten

1 teaspoon white vinegar

2 tablespoons ice water

¾ cup (1½ sticks) cold unsalted butter, cut into pieces

1 egg + a few drops of water beaten together, for egg wash

¼ cup raw turbinado sugar + ½ teaspoon cinnamon, for serving

apple filling

2 large Honeycrisp apples, thinly sliced

1½ tablespoons cornstarch

1½ tablespoons granulated sugar

1 teaspoon ground ginger

½ teaspoon ground cinnamon

¼ teaspoon ground cardamom

¼ teaspoon ground nutmeg

Pinch of kosher salt

10-Minute Meal Prep

The crust can be made a few days ahead of time and stored in the fridge. It can also be stored in the freezer for up to 6 weeks. The caramel sauce can be made ahead of time and stored in the fridge for 2 to 3 days.

I came from a long line of women whose culinary success lay in their piecrust. And let's just say I did not inherit the piccrust gene.

Even though I spent hours in the kitchen with my grandma while she baked, she baked by look, feel, and touch and rarely followed a recipe. Her crust was flaky and wonderful every single time. She was patient. The fillings were perfect! And she was passionate about it.

I, on the other hand? Am not passionate about it. I don't love pushing piecrust into a plate, crimping the edges and making it look pretty.

What I do love, though, is making said crust into a rustic galette. Rolling it out until it's a giant slab with jagged edges, filling the center with fruit or even vegetables, and folding up those sides until it's a cute little pie pocket that's ready to bake.

It's the best of both worlds: no fussy piecrust, with all the benefits of the pie flavor. You still get to eat pie without it being pie!

And I do use my grandma's piecrust recipe, so that has to be good for something. Here, I fill it with thinly sliced apples and warming spices, then bake it until the crust is golden and crunchy.

I finish off everything with a drizzle of spiced caramel. A cozy, inviting slice is calling your name.

---

make the galette crust Add the flour, granulated sugar, cinnamon, and salt to a food processor and pulse just until combined. In a small bowl, whisk together the egg, vinegar, and water. Add the cold butter pieces to the food processor and pulse until small, coarse crumbs remain. Sprinkle the vinegar-egg mixture over the flour and pulse again until the dough comes together.

Remove the dough with your hands and wrap it in plastic wrap. Refrigerate the dough for 30 minutes. After 30 minutes, preheat the oven to 400°F.

make the apple filling Place the apples in a large bowl. Sprinkle with the cornstarch, sugar, spices, and salt. Toss the apples well and let them sit for 10 minutes.

ingredients and recipe continue

easy everyday

spiced caramel sauce

½ cup granulated sugar

½ cup packed brown sugar

6 tablespoons unsalted butter

½ cup heavy cream

½ teaspoon ground cinnamon

½ teaspoon ground ginger

¼ teaspoon ground cardamom

¼ teaspoon kosher salt

1 tablespoon pure vanilla extract

make the spiced caramel sauce   Combine the sugars, butter, cream, spices, and salt in a saucepan over medium heat. Cook for 5 to 6 minutes, stirring often, so there are no lumps and the caramel doesn't bubble over. Once thickened, turn off the heat. Whisk the vanilla into the caramel.

make the galette   Line a baking sheet with parchment paper. Remove the crust from the fridge. Roll it into a rustic almost-circle shape until it is about ¼ inch thick. Place the dough on the parchment-lined baking sheet.

Layer the apples in the center, leaving a 2-inch border of crust. Drizzle the apples with 2 tablespoons of the caramel sauce. Fold the crust over the top of the apples. Brush the crust with the egg wash. Sprinkle any of the exposed crust with the cinnamon and turbinado sugar mixture. Bake the galette until the crust is golden, 40 to 45 minutes.

Remove from the heat and let cool slightly. Pour into a jar and let cool completely. Store in the fridge for 1 to 2 weeks.

meyer lemon pudding cake

¾ cup granulated sugar

⅓ cup all-purpose flour

¼ teaspoon kosher salt

3 large eggs, separated

2 tablespoons unsalted butter, melted and slightly cooled

1 cup whole milk

2 tablespoons finely grated Meyer lemon zest

5 tablespoons fresh Meyer lemon juice

Confectioners' sugar, for serving

This pudding cake looks like nothing but tastes like everything. While you're mixing it, you will think, "Wow, this looks boring." Because it just doesn't seem impressive. When you fold in the whipped egg whites, you'll be skeptical again. How could something that looks this plain taste so good?

Well, let me tell you. This is a fluffy, soufflé-like cake that is filled with a faux lemon curd. It's like a tender cake sitting on lemon pudding and it's the eyes-roll-back-in-your-head kind of good.

Add some confectioners' sugar, sliced almonds, or raspberries if you want to make it look pretty. But trust me, it doesn't even need it.

Preheat the oven to 350°F. Liberally spray a 9-inch pie plate with nonstick spray.

In a large bowl, whisk together the granulated sugar, flour, and salt.

In another large bowl, whisk together the egg yolks and melted butter. Whisk in the milk and the lemon zest and juice until combined. Stir in the dry ingredients.

Beat the egg whites in the bowl of a stand mixer until stiff peaks form. Slowly fold the egg whites into the lemon mixture, gently, just until combined. Do not stir, just fold. Pour the batter into the pie plate.

Bake for 30 to 35 minutes, until set. Top with confectioners' sugar and serve!

10-Minute Meal Prep

The ingredients can be measured out ahead of time and stored in the fridge.

apple cider donut snack cake

2 cups all-purpose flour

1½ tablespoons baking powder

2 teaspoons cinnamon

1 teaspoon kosher salt

½ teaspoon allspice

¼ teaspoon nutmeg

¾ cup granulated sugar

¾ cup loosely packed brown sugar

½ cup (1 stick) unsalted butter, melted and cooled

2 large eggs

2 teaspoons pure vanilla extract

½ cup applesauce

½ cup apple cider

topping

2 tablespoons unsalted butter, melted

1 teaspoon cinnamon

1 tablespoon sugar

Apple cider donuts are the best donuts. There, I said it.

I wait all year long for apple cider donuts. I don't even really like cake donuts, but there is something about apple cider donuts that reel me in. I can't escape.

Their fluffy, spiced interior with that golden apple flavor? Oh man. It's like the first bite of fall on a cool, sunny day, leaves crunching under your feet while you finish the donut. Covered in spiced sugar that sticks to your face with each bite, the apple cider donut flavor is one I chase all year long, hoping to get just one more bite before the season ends.

This snack cake is small and fluffy, topped with melted butter and that spiced sugar we love so much. The texture is almost like your favorite cake donut.

And let's be real: Calling it a snack cake just makes it appropriate for breakfast. Have a slice for breakfast!

Preheat the oven to 350°F. Spray a 9 × 13-inch baking dish with nonstick baking spray.

In a small bowl, whisk together the flour, baking powder, cinnamon, salt, allspice, and nutmeg.

In a large bowl, whisk together both sugars and the butter. Whisk in each egg, one at a time. Whisk in the vanilla and applesauce.

Stir in half of the dry ingredients. Stir in the apple cider. Stir in the remaining dry ingredients just until combined.

Bake the cake for 28 to 32 minutes, or until a tester inserted in the center comes out clean.

Let cool, then brush the cake with the melted butter. Sprinkle with the cinnamon sugar topping. Slice and serve.

10-Minute Meal Prep

The ingredients can be measured out ahead of time, dry ingredients combined and cold ingredients stored in the fridge until ready to use.

easy everyday

no bake s'mores pie

1½ cups graham cracker crumbs, plus extra for serving

½ cup (1 stick) salted butter, melted

16 ounces milk or dark chocolate (your preference!), chopped

2 cups heavy cream

½ cup (1 stick) unsalted butter, at room temperature, cut into pieces

4 large egg whites

1 cup sugar

½ teaspoon cream of tartar

2 teaspoons pure vanilla extract

I freakishly love pies with a graham cracker crust. Maybe it's because I have such an aversion to the classic pie dough, but a graham cracker crust is so buttery. So crunchy. I love the base it provides to any pie and I much prefer it over flaky layers.

This pie can be made ahead of time, with its silky filling and textured crust. It's best stored in the fridge of course but bring it out a few minutes before serving and slicing. It's a little slice of bliss.

In a bowl, combine the graham cracker crumbs and melted butter. Stir until combined and the crumbs are all moistened. Press the mixture in a 9-inch pie plate to form a crust. Stick the crust in the fridge while you make the filling.

Place the chocolate in a large bowl. Heat the heavy cream in a saucepan over medium-low heat, until just hot but not bubbling. Pour the cream over the chopped chocolate. Let sit for 1 to 2 minutes without stirring. After 2 minutes, stir continuously until the chocolate is smooth and a ganache comes together. Stir in the butter until completely melted.

Pour the chocolate ganache into the piecrust, smoothing out the top. Place the pie dish back in the fridge for at least 2 hours, or overnight.

To make the marshmallow frosting, combine the egg whites, sugar, and cream of tartar in a heat-proof bowl, preferably the bowl of a stand mixer. Place over the top of a double-boiler that contains simmering water, and whisk constantly for 3 to 4 minutes until the sugar has dissolved and the egg whites are slightly warm. Immediately remove the bowl and place it on your stand mixer with the whisk attachment, beating slowly at first and gradually increasing the speed to high.

Beat for 6 to 7 minutes until glossy and thick, then beat in the vanilla for another minute, until combined. Pile the frosting on top of the ganache before serving. You can do this 1 to 2 hours ahead of time. Sprinkle with graham cracker crumbs, slice, and serve!

10-Minute Meal Prep

The crust can be made ahead of time and stored in the fridge for 1 to 2 days. The crust can also be finished with the ganache a day or two ahead of time, covered, and stored in the fridge until ready to top with the frosting.

pumpkin toffee dream cake

2 cups all-purpose flour

2 teaspoons baking soda

1¼ teaspoons cinnamon

½ teaspoon kosher salt

¼ teaspoon freshly grated nutmeg

15 ounces pumpkin puree

1¾ cups packed brown sugar

½ cup plain Greek yogurt

½ cup vegetable oil

4 large eggs

2 teaspoons pure vanilla extract

toffee cream cheese frosting

8 ounces cream cheese, at room temperature

½ cup (1 stick) unsalted butter, at room temperature

2½ cups confectioners' sugar

2 teaspoons pure vanilla extract

⅓ cup shaved milk chocolate curls, for serving

⅓ cup toffee bits, for serving

This is my most famous cake, with an upgrade.

My pumpkin dream cake is fluffy and light with the perfect tender crumb. The flavor is incredible. I don't like a ton of spice with my pumpkin, so if you do, double the spices here.

To add something special, throw crushed toffee bits on top. The chocolatey crunch mixed with the pumpkin is just what this dish needs!

Preheat the oven to 350°F. Spray a 9 × 13-inch baking dish with nonstick baking spray.

In a large bowl, whisk together the flour, baking soda, cinnamon, salt, and nutmeg. Note: If you LOVE spice, feel free to add some extra spice in here (pumpkin! allspice! more cinnamon!—you can add another ½ to 1 teaspoon if you'd like), as this isn't overly spiced.

In another large bowl, whisk together the pumpkin puree, brown sugar, yogurt, and oil. Once smooth and combined, whisk in each egg, one at a time. Whisk in the vanilla.

Add the dry ingredients to the wet, mixing until combined and no large lumps remain.

Pour the batter into the greased baking dish. Bake for 30 to 35 minutes, or until a tester inserted in the center of the cake comes out clean.

Cool the cake completely.

make the cream cheese frosting   Beat the cream cheese and butter together until creamy. Beat in the confectioners' sugar until combined and smooth. Beat on high for 2 to 3 minutes, scraping down the bottom of the bowl. Beat in the vanilla. Frost the cooled cake. Top with the chocolate shavings and toffee bits. Refrigerate the cake or any leftovers. The cake will keep for up to a week in the fridge!

10-Minute Meal Prep

The ingredients can be measured ahead of time and stored in the fridge. The frosting can be made ahead of time and stored in the fridge for 2 to 3 days, but must come to room temperature before frosting.

cherry cheesecake puff pastry turnovers

4 ounces cream cheese, softened

2 tablespoons confectioners' sugar, plus extra for serving

1 teaspoon pure vanilla extract

2 sheets puff pastry, thawed if frozen

1 cup cherry pie filling

1 egg + 1 teaspoon water, beaten together for egg wash

vanilla glaze

½ cup confectioners' sugar

¼ teaspoon pure vanilla extract

1 tablespoon heavy cream

1 tablespoon milk, plus extra if needed

Welcome back, puff pastry! I'm so glad you're here.

Puff pastry isn't just for use with savory items in my kitchen. Here, I make little pockets and fill them with classic cherry pie filling and a cheesecake mixture that is absolutely delicious. It's certainly semi-homemade, but there is just something about how wonderful a sour cherry filling is inside baked goods. Sour cherries are near impossible to find in my area, so I like to use a pie filling for these when I need to make a super-quick treat. Everyone LOVES these.

These pockets get baked until the cherry filling is exploding, and you'll have a magic pocket filled with sweet cherry cheesecake goodness.

Sign me up.

Preheat the oven to 425°F. Line a baking sheet with parchment paper.

Place the cream cheese in a bowl. Add the sugar and vanilla. Beat with an electric mixer until combined and creamy, about 5 minutes.

Cut each sheet of puff pastry into eight pieces. In the center of one, add 2 to 3 tablespoons of the cream cheese mixture. Add 2 to 3 tablespoons of the cherry filling. Brush the edges with the egg wash. Top with a piece of the puff pastry and press the edges together with a fork to seal them. Repeat with the remaining squares.

Brush the puff pastry with the egg wash. Place the sheet in the oven and bake for 20 to 25 minutes, until golden brown. Let cool for 5 to 10 minutes. Sprinkle with confectioners' sugar. Drizzle with the vanilla glaze.

make the vanilla glaze Whisk together the sugar, vanilla, cream, and milk until smooth. If the mixture is still too thick, whisk in more milk, 1 teaspoon at a time.

10-Minute Meal Prep

The cream cheese filling can be made ahead of time and stored in the fridge until ready to use.

banana bundt cake with espresso glaze

3 cups all-purpose flour

2 teaspoons baking soda

½ teaspoon kosher salt

1 teaspoon cinnamon

1 cup (2 sticks) unsalted butter, at room temperature

1½ cups granulated sugar

2 large eggs

2 teaspoons pure vanilla extract

1½ cups mashed ripe bananas (about 4 bananas)

1 cup plain Greek yogurt

espresso glaze

1½ cups confectioners' sugar

1 teaspoon instant espresso powder

2 ounces freshly brewed espresso

1 teaspoon milk, plus more for thinning

½ teaspoon pure vanilla extract

This flavor combo—banana bread and coffee—is one for the books.

A classic banana bread turned into a Bundt cake might be the best shape of cake, don't you think? And blanketed by an espresso glaze.

The glaze gives a richness to the banana bread while still letting the classic flavor shine. And it's a fun way to switch it up from traditional bread. I'd take a slice of this any day.

Preheat the oven to 350°F. Spray a 12-cup Bundt pan with nonstick baking spray, making sure the inside is fully covered. Be sure to use baking spray—the kind with the flour in it.

In a large bowl, combine the flour, baking soda, salt, and cinnamon.

In the bowl of a stand mixer, beat together the butter and granulated sugar until combined and creamy, about 5 minutes. Beat in the eggs one at a time. Scrape the bottom and the sides of the bowl as needed. Beat in the vanilla.

Beat in the mashed bananas. Beat in half of the dry ingredients and the Greek yogurt. Beat in the remaining dry ingredients, making sure everything is combined.

Pour the mixture into the prepared Bundt pan. Bake for 50 to 55 minutes, or until the center of the cake is set. Let cool for 30 minutes, then invert the pan and let the cake cool completely.

make the espresso glaze   Whisk together the confectioners' sugar, espresso powder, espresso, milk, and vanilla until a smooth, drippy glaze forms. If the mixture is too thin, you can thicken it by adding a little more confectioners' sugar. If it seems too thick, add 1 teaspoon of milk at a time, whisking to combine. Pour it over the banana Bundt and let it set for 20 minutes before slicing.

10-Minute Meal Prep

All the ingredients can be measured ahead of time and stored in the fridge before baking.

brown butter snickerdoodle blondies

2 cups all-purpose flour

1 teaspoon cinnamon

½ teaspoon baking soda

½ teaspoon kosher salt

½ teaspoon cream of tartar

1 cup (2 sticks) unsalted butter

1½ cups light brown sugar, loosely packed

2 eggs, lightly beaten

1 tablespoon pure vanilla extract

½ cup granulated sugar +
1 teaspoon cinnamon, for serving

Hello and welcome to your new favorite cookie bar! Think classic cookie bar meets snickerdoodle—that's what we have going on here.

There is tons of cinnamon sugar. The bars also have a slight tang, just like the classic, original snickerdoodle you know and love.

And these bars have the perfect amount of chew!

They are impossible to resist.

Preheat the oven to 350°F.

In a small bowl, whisk together the flour, cinnamon, baking soda, salt, and cream of tartar.

Place the butter in a skillet over medium heat. Cook and let the mixture bubble, stirring occasionally, until brown bits begin to appear on the bottom. Once the brown bits appear, turn off the heat and continue to stir for about 30 seconds. Let the butter cool slightly. Take a pastry brush and brush a bit of the butter all over the bottom and sides of a 9 × 13-inch baking dish.

Place the brown sugar in a large bowl. Pour the rest of the butter in the brown butter and mix until combined and smooth—the sugar will somewhat dissolve. Add the eggs one at a time, stirring immediately after so they don't cook if the butter is still warm. Stir in the vanilla.

Stir in the dry ingredients until they are almost combined.

Press the mixture into the buttered dish. Sprinkle the cinnamon-sugar mixture on top. Bake for 25 to 30 minutes, or until the top is golden brown and set in the center. Let cool completely before slicing into squares.

10-Minute Meal Prep

The ingredients can all be measured out ahead of time and stored in the fridge until ready to bake.

sour cream peach cobbler

peach filling

6 tablespoons unsalted butter, cut into pieces

4 cups sliced peaches (6 large ripe peaches)

1 cup granulated sugar

¼ cup all-purpose flour

Pinch of kosher salt

2 tablespoons freshly squeezed lemon juice

topping

1 cup all-purpose flour

¼ cup granulated sugar

2½ teaspoons baking powder

½ teaspoon kosher salt

2 tablespoons unsalted butter, melted and cooled

1 cup sour cream

⅓ cup heavy cream

1 tablespoon pure vanilla extract

Turbinado sugar

Vanilla ice cream, for serving

We didn't eat a lot of peach cobbler when I was growing up. But I distinctly remember my mom making it once or twice in the summer. And we all loved it. Hers was made with canned peaches and a box mix, and as soon as I perfected this recipe, I knew we could never eat it the old way again.

The cobbler part of this recipe includes sour cream, which brings a tenderness to the crumb and adds the perfect amount of moisture. The topping is more like a cake than a crumble, and it's a lovely vehicle for vanilla ice cream. This recipe also works with berries and pears, too!

Preheat the oven to 375°F. Place the butter pieces all over a 9 × 13-inch baking dish.

make the peach filling In the buttered baking dish, mix together the peaches, granulated sugar, flour, and salt, then sprinkle on the lemon juice. Toss everything together well until the sugar is moistened and all the peaches are covered. Let sit while you make the topping.

make the topping In a small bowl, whisk together the flour, granulated sugar, baking powder, and salt.

Place the melted butter in a large bowl. Mix in the sour cream—this will take a minute to come together. You can use a whisk, spatula, or wooden spoon. Mix in the heavy cream and vanilla until combined.

Mix in the dry ingredients until fully combined. Drop the batter by the spoonful all over the peaches. Sprinkle the batter with a little bit of turbinado sugar.

Bake for 55 to 60 minutes, or until the topping is golden brown and cooked through. Let cool slightly before serving with ice cream.

10-Minute Meal Prep

All the ingredients can be measured out and stored in the fridge before baking.

chewy caramel pretzel cookies

3 cups all-purpose flour

1 teaspoon baking soda

½ teaspoon baking powder

1 teaspoon sea salt

1 cup (2 sticks) salted butter, softened

1 cup granulated sugar

1 cup packed light brown sugar

2 large eggs

2 teaspoons pure vanilla extract

1 cup caramel squares, unwrapped

1 cup crushed pretzels

Pretzel twists, for topping (optional)

There's a little cookie shop in Harbor Springs, Michigan, called Tom's Mom's Cookies. And the cookies are incredible. Big, chewy, soft, and utterly perfect.

My favorite cookie on the list the last few years has been their caramel pretzel cookie. And it is such a lovely mix of crunchy, salty pretzels and caramel bites and pulls that I never thought I would be able to re-create it.

But I was wrong!

These caramel pretzel cookies are just as divine. Mini pretzels and square caramels are stirred into cookie dough and baked. The round bites of love are filled with stretches of chewy caramel, salty pretzel chunks throughout, and an overall buttery, almost butterscotch vibe. They might be my favorite cookie, period.

Preheat the oven to 375°F. In a large bowl, whisk together the flour, baking soda, baking powder, and salt. Line a baking sheet with parchment paper.

Beat the butter and both sugars together with an electric mixer for about 5 minutes, until fluffy. Beat in the eggs one at a time until combined. Beat in the vanilla, scraping the bottom and sides of the bowl as needed.

Add the dry ingredients and mix until just combined. Stir in the caramels and the crushed pretzels with a spatula.

Scoop the dough into 2 or 3 tablespoon-size portions on the parchment-lined baking sheet at least 2 inches apart. If desired, you can press a pretzel twist into the center of the dough. Bake for 8 to 10 minutes, until just barely baked through.

Let cool completely before removing from the pan.

I like to scoop this dough into balls and freeze for up to 3 months, then have them on hand at any time to bake straight from the freezer.

10-Minute Meal Prep

All the ingredients can be measured before baking. The caramels can also be unwrapped and the pretzels can be crushed ahead of time.

my grandma's frozen cranberry slice

1 cup heavy cream

3 ounces cream cheese, softened

2 tablespoons plain Greek yogurt

2 tablespoons sugar

1 cup chopped fresh pineapple

15 ounces whole-berry cranberry sauce

½ cup chopped pistachios

¼ cup chopped dark chocolate, plus additional for serving

We're throwing it back to a retro recipe here that my grandma used to serve every holiday season. Just the sight of this cranberry slice brings me all the nostalgic memories, and it feels like yesterday when I sat at her meticulously set dining table with a slice of this on my plate.

This dessert is made ahead of time, pressed into a loaf pan, and frozen. The key is using a piece of parchment paper in the pan, which allows you to lift up the loaf from the pan.

It's sweet and almost marshmallowy, reminiscent of ice cream, and also tart with bites of cranberry.

I've added a few special touches that I think make a difference here (pistachios!) and occasionally toss in some shaved dark chocolate.

It might taste like the nineties, but in the very best way possible.

Place a sheet of parchment paper in a 9 × 5-inch loaf pan. Let the edges hang over, folding them against the sides.

Place the heavy cream in the bowl of a stand mixer. Beat on medium speed until peaks form, 4 to 5 minutes, and the cream is whipped. Set aside.

Place the cream cheese, yogurt, and sugar in the bowl of a food processor. Blend until the mixture is smooth and combined. Add the pineapple and pulse a few times, until the pineapple is finely chopped. Add the cranberry sauce and pulse a few more times.

Transfer the mixture to a bowl. Fold in the pistachios. Fold in the whipped cream until the mixture is lighter in color, fluffy, and combined. Fold in the dark chocolate.

Press the mixture into the loaf pan. Cover with plastic wrap and freeze for at least 6 hours, or overnight.

Remove and use the parchment sides to lift the mixture from the pan. Use a sharp knife to cut it into slices. Serve!

10-Minute Meal Prep

The cream can be whipped 2 to 4 hours ahead of time and stored in the fridge in a sealed container.

CHAPTER 7

cocktails &
mocktails

If you're in need of the perfect party punch or a lovely lemonade to serve at a summer barbecue, you're in the right spot.

Margaritas, mojitos, and spritzes are some of my favorite drinks to serve in the summer. As soon as a chill hits the air, I move into simmered spices, red wine–based cocktails, and warming ginger beer mocktails.

I've always loved experimenting with drinks, and here you'll find ten of my favorite drinks. Five of them are boozy and five are nonalcoholic, making it easy to choose one for whoever you're hosting!

Special signature drinks have always made my parties feel more personal. These drink recipes add an extra touch, and it doesn't always have to be a drink filled with booze. Sure, Red Wine Cider Sangria (page 233) is perfect for Thanksgiving, but making a batch of my Coconut Beach Quenchers (page 242) to stay hydrated at a summer pool party is also super fun. Even a coffee or hot chocolate bar, complete with chocolate and peppermint stirrers, marshmallows, and sugar cubes can make things feel festive.

It's also not difficult to leave the alcohol out of the boozy options here, which is a nice touch! Swap in extra club soda for the gin or tequila. It's as easy as that! ●

cherry aperol spritz

Orange wedge, for serving

Maraschino cherries, for serving

6 ounces Aperol

2 ounces maraschino cherry juice

8 ounces dry prosecco

1 ounce club soda (plain or citrus flavor)

In this drink, I combine two of my favorite things: Aperol spritzes and maraschino cherries.

I don't care if spritzes are out these days, or if they were "in" a mere five years ago. They will ALWAYS be in for me because they are one of my favorite cocktails. I love having one of these refreshing, citrusy, and pretty drinks on vacation.

For this version, I add some maraschino cherry juice to the classic and drop in some cherries. Maraschino cherries are a nostalgic treat for me, and occasionally I love to include them in some of my more modern recipes.

This is super fun and beautiful, complete with sweetness, a slight bitter hint from the Aperol, and a citrusy twist. Delish!

Fill two wineglasses with crushed ice, cherries, and an orange wedge. Fill each with 3 ounces of Aperol. Add an ounce of cherry juice in each. Add 4 ounces of prosecco to each. Top with the club soda. Serve!

red wine cider sangria

2 apples, sliced

2 pears, sliced

1 orange, thinly sliced

4 cinnamon sticks

1 (750mL) bottle pinot noir, chilled

2 cups cold apple cider

½ cup orange liqueur

3 tablespoons pure maple syrup

As soon as the calendar turns to September 1, this sangria becomes my signature drink. From that moment until January, you'll find me serving this red wine sangria, made with apple cider, cinnamon sticks, orange liqueur, and loads of fruit. It is everyone's favorite for a reason!

In the bottom of a pitcher, add the apples, pears, oranges, and cinnamon sticks. Pour in the wine, apple cider, orange liqueur, and maple syrup. Stir to mix. Stick it in the fridge for 30 minutes to marry everything together before serving.

10-Minute Meal Prep

You can prepare the sangria the night before, but do not add the cinnamon sticks until 1 hour before serving.

gingerbread espresso martini

gingerbread syrup

½ cup water

½ cup brown sugar

1 tablespoon molasses

½ teaspoon cinnamon

1 pinch freshly grated nutmeg

½ teaspoon ginger

espresso martini

4 ounces vodka

2 ounces espresso

2 ounces gingerbread syrup

2 ounces coffee liqueur

2 ounces Irish cream liqueur

Gingerbread cookies, for serving

I will never get over just how much I love espresso martinis. But there is a time and place to drink them, and I rarely want to be up all night after consuming caffeine late in the day. My preference is to make these at happy hour and even use decaf coffee if possible.

This gingerbread version is spiced and flavorful, with cinnamon, nutmeg, and ginger. Shaking the drink makes it foamy on top, giving that milk cloud feel. I love to serve these at a cookie decorating or gingerbread house party, as well as on Christmas Eve (although there's no reason you can't enjoy this at other times of the year). You can also use the gingerbread syrup in coffee!

make the gingerbread syrup Combine the water, brown sugar, molasses, cinnamon, nutmeg, and ginger in a saucepan over medium-low heat. Whisk until the sugar dissolves. Boil the mixture for 1 minute, then turn off the heat and continue to whisk for another 30 seconds. Transfer the syrup to a jar. Let it cool completely before using or refrigerating.

make the martini In a cocktail shaker, combine the vodka, espresso, gingerbread syrup, and liqueurs. Shake for 30 seconds, until frothy and mixed, then evenly divide between two chilled martini glasses. Garnish with a cookie and serve!

10-Minute Meal Prep

The syrup can be made ahead of time and stored in the fridge for 3 to 4 days.

pomegranate paloma

2 ounces Blanco tequila

2 ounces pomegranate juice

2 ounces freshly squeezed lime juice

8 ounces grapefruit soda, such as Fresca

Lime wedges, for serving

Grapefruit wheels, for serving

Pomegranate arils, for serving

Tequila is my favorite liquor and usually my drink of choice, so I love any cocktails that include it. Margaritas, of course, are up there for me. But a classic paloma, with lots of grapefruit and lime, is one of my favorite drinks of all time.

Here, I like to put a tart and punchy spin on it, adding pomegranate juice and grapefruit soda, making it taste more full bodied with a hint of berry. I still keep the citrus wedge and also add a few pops of pomegranate arils. It makes for a stunning presentation.

Fill two highball glasses with crushed ice. Add 1 ounce each of the tequila, pomegranate juice, and lime juice to each glass. Fill to the top with the grapefruit soda and stir. Garnish with lime wedges, grapefruit wheels, and pomegranate arils.

strawberry gin smash

strawberry sauce

1 cup fresh strawberries, chopped

¼ cup sugar

gin smash

4 ounces gin

1 ounce freshly squeezed lime juice

8 ounces club soda

Mint sprigs, for serving

Lime wedges, for serving

Strawberries, for serving

Fresh fruit made me fall in love with gin cocktails. I find that berries, peaches, and citrus are my go-to, and they make the drink super refreshing and enjoyable for me.

Fresh strawberries, muddled and dropped in with the ice cubes, add a sweet spin to the botanical gin and fizzy soda in this version. It's light and easy, excellent on a hot summer day or lovely at a brunch with friends.

make the strawberry sauce Combine the strawberries and sugar in a saucepan over medium heat. Cook, stirring often, until bubbly and saucy, 10 to 12 minutes. Use a wooden spoon to smash the strawberries. Remove the pan from the heat and pour the strawberries into a jar. Let cool completely before using or refrigerating.

make the gin smash Fill two highball glasses with 2 tablespoons each of the strawberry base. Top with crushed ice. Pour 2 ounces of the gin into each glass, then ½ ounce of the lime juice into each. Stir. Top with the club soda. Garnish with a mint sprig, lime wedge, and strawberries.

10-Minute Meal Prep

The strawberry base can be made ahead of time and stored in the fridge for 3 to 4 days.

cranberry citrus spritzers

½ cup 100% cranberry juice

½ cup freshly squeezed orange juice

½ cup lemon-lime soda

1 cup citrus-flavored seltzer water

2 orange wheels, for serving

4 mint sprigs, for serving

This winter beauty is refreshing and light, lovely served with a sprig of rosemary and enjoyed next to a holiday cheese board. It's tart, citrusy, and smells like heavenly orange. Top it off with a cranberry- or mandarin-flavored seltzer and it's the ideal winter mocktail.

Fill four glasses with crushed ice.

Stir together the juices and soda. Divide evenly over ice in each glass. Top each with ¼ cup of the seltzer water. Add half an orange wheel and a mint sprig for garnish.

coconut beach quencher

1 cup coconut water

1 cup pineapple juice

¼ cup freshly squeezed orange juice

¼ cup canned coconut cream

2 tablespoons freshly squeezed lime juice

Fresh pineapple slices and berries, for serving

This coconut water–based mocktail is perfectly served over ice, taken to the pool or beach, and garnished with tons of fresh, seasonal fruit. It reminds me of a painkiller cocktail, which is made with pineapple juice, orange juice, and coconut cream—and is one of my most favorite cocktails ever.

It's hydrating, beautiful, and delicious all at the same time.

Stir or shake together in a cocktail shaker the coconut water, pineapple juice, orange juice, coconut cream, and lime juice.

Fill four glasses with crushed ice. Divide the drink evenly among the glasses. Garnish with fresh pineapple and berries.

Serves 2 | Time: 30 minutes

frozen lavender lemonade

lavender syrup

½ cup sugar

½ cup water

2 teaspoons dried culinary lavender

½ teaspoon pure vanilla extract

lemonade

2 tablespoons fresh lemon zest

½ cup freshly squeezed lemon juice

⅓ cup lavender syrup

4 cups ice cubes

Lavender sprigs, for serving

Frozen lemonade is one of summer's best treats. Refreshing and icy, it hits the spot and quenches your thirst. This lemonade is infused with fresh lavender and mint. I love using lavender with lemon—and mixing it with sugar. It takes on a fancy, elegant dessert-like flavor and infuses the drink without making it taste like a bouquet of flowers. There is no better way to make your glass of lemonade feel "grown up."

make the lavender syrup   Place the sugar, water, and lavender in a saucepan over medium-low heat. Whisk until the sugar dissolves, bringing the mixture to a simmer. Cook for 1 minute. Turn off the heat and set the saucepan aside. Let it cool completely. Strain the mixture through a fine-mesh sieve to remove the lavender. Stir in the vanilla. See 10-Minute tip.

make the lemonade   Blend together the lemon zest and juice, lavender syrup, and ice cubes until frosty. Divide evenly between two glasses. Garnish with fresh lavender sprigs.

10-Minute Meal Prep

The lavender syrup can be made ahead of time and stored in the fridge for 3 to 4 days.

spiced winter cider

16 ounces apple cider

8 ounces pomegranate juice
(use 100% juice, not a cocktail)

8 ounces water

½ cup loosely packed brown sugar,
plus more as needed

3 cinnamon sticks

2 star anise

1 to 2 cardamom pods

Orange rind, from 1 orange

½ cup freshly squeezed orange juice

For serving: whipped cream,
cinnamon sticks, pomegranate arils
(optional)

Otherwise known as a hug in a mug!

When you're craving a cup of something warm and cozy, this is your girl. Cider simmered with anise, cinnamon sticks, and cardamom, poured into a glass, and topped with soft whipped cream, is quite possibly the best thing you can drink while sitting next to the fire.

It warms you to your soul. It tastes delicious, like happy holiday memories and firewood smoke and pine trees and arctic snow.

Make a big batch of this in a slow cooker for a party, or just make a single cup to enjoy while you sit with your favorite book. Now isn't that a dream come true?

In a saucepan, combine the cider, juice, water, brown sugar, cinnamon sticks, star anise, cardamom, orange rind, and orange juice. Bring to a boil, then cover and reduce to a simmer. Simmer for 15 minutes.

Uncover and taste. If it's too tart and needs more sweetness, whisk in a bit more sugar, about ¼ cup, and simmer for a few more minutes.

Strain out the cinnamon sticks, star anise, cardamom, and orange rind and discard. Ladle the cider into mugs. If desired, serve topped with whipped cream and garnished with cinnamon sticks and pomegranate arils.

10-Minute Meal Prep

The ingredients can be measured out a day ahead of time and stored in the fridge until ready to use.

0%

blackberry ginger beer

blackberry sauce

8 ounces blackberries

⅓ cup sugar

½ ounce freshly squeezed lemon juice

ginger beer

6 ounces ginger beer or ginger ale

½ ounce freshly squeezed lime juice

Splash of lime seltzer

¼ cup blackberries, for serving

Mint sprigs, for serving

Lime wedges, for serving

I adore ginger beer because even serving a glass of it alone, over ice, makes it feel special. It is so spicy and, well, for lack of a better word—GINGERY. The bite that comes from one sip is something I crave and, mixed with the bubbles and a bit of fruit, this tastes like a super-fancy drink.

make the blackberry sauce Combine the berries, sugar, and lemon juice in a saucepan over medium heat. Cook, stirring often, until the blackberries break down and the mixture is bubbly, about 10 minutes. Sometimes I use a wooden spoon to smash the berries. When the blackberries are broken, remove the sauce from the heat and pour it in a jar. Let cool completely before using or refrigerating.

make the ginger beer To make the drink, add 2 tablespoons of the blackberry puree in each highball glass. Add crushed ice on top. Pour in the ginger beer, lime juice, and seltzer. Add the fresh blackberries and stir. Garnish with a sprig of fresh mint and a lime wedge.

10-Minute Meal Prep

The blackberry puree can be made ahead of time and stored in the fridge for 3 to 4 days until ready to use.

acknowledgments

To all my internet BFFs, the ones who have read *How Sweet Eats* from the beginning, where we've cheered one another on at the dinner table, THANK YOU. This whole entire thing would not even exist without you, and I value you more than you know. I appreciate your support so much!

Stacey, I cannot thank you enough for being the best agent and sounding board, for listening to my freak-outs, and always being my biggest supportive and cheerleader. No one believes in me like you do! You are one of my favorite people!!

Dervla! I am so honored to be working on another book with you. You are the best of the best and I feel lucky to call you my editor and friend. Your attention to detail is impeccable and I value your opinion more than anything. Thank you for making the book writing process such a fun and enjoyable experience!

Thank you to Katherine, Jenny, Amy, Kelly, Kevin, and the entire team at Penguin Random House for the endless hours of work to bring this book together. Especially with how wordy I am.

Thank you to all my incredible recipe testers who made dish after dish. Special thanks to Donnelle and Randi for your extraordinary help!

Lacy, I couldn't do any of this without you. You are my go-to source for everything food (and life!) and I trust your opinion and taste more than anyone else. I am so thankful and thrilled we get to do this together!

Alex, you are the reason I can do what I do. I would not survive without your support and thank God every day that you came into our life.

Mom & Dad, thank you for getting us around the dinner table nearly every single night when I was a kid. It's forever embedded in my soul.

To my amazing family, the loves of my life. Eddie, Max, Emilia, and Jordan, you are my muses, my world, my everything. Thank you for eating so many different dishes when all you want is a "regular meal." I love our wonderful little life and can't believe you are all mine. It's everything I've ever wanted and more.

index